THE CHEMICAL WEDDING OF CHRISTIAN ROSENKREUTZ

Chymische Hoch-
zeit:
Christiani Rosencreütz.

ANNO 1459.

Arcana publicata vilescunt; & gra-
tiam prophanata amittunt.

Ergo: ne Margaritas obijce porcis, seu
Asino substerne rosas.

Straßburg,
In Verlegung / Lazari Zetzners.
Anno M. DC. XVI.

THE CHEMICAL WEDDING OF CHRISTIAN ROSENKREUTZ

TRANSLATED BY
JOSCELYN GODWIN

INTRODUCTION AND COMMENTARY
BY ADAM MCLEAN

MAGNUM OPUS HERMETIC SOURCEWORKS #18

PHANES PRESS

This work, part of the Magnum Opus Hermetic Sourceworks series, was previously published in a hardbound edition, limited to 250 copies, in 1984. This edition contains a new translation of the *Chemical Wedding*, which did not appear in the earlier version. The Magnum Opus Hermetic Sourceworks series is published under the General Editorship of Adam McLean.

Published by Phanes Press and distributed by Red Wheel/Weiser, LLC
368 Congress Street, Fourth Floor, Boston, Massachusetts 02210
www.weiser.com

09 08 07 06 05   10 9 8 7 6 5 4 3

Library of Congress Cataloging-in-Publication Data

Rosenkreutz, Christian.
    [Chymische Hochzeit. English]
    The Chemical wedding of Christian Rosenkreutz / translated by
Jocelyn Godwin ; introduction and commentary by Adam McLean.
       p.   cm. — [Magnum Opus Hermetic Sourceworks ; no. 18]
    Translation of: Chymische Hochzeit.
    ISBN 0-933999-34-8 (cloth : alk. paper)—ISBN 0-933999-35-6
(pbk.: alk paper)
    1. Society of Rosicrucians. 2. Rosenkreutz, Christian. 3. Chymische
Hochzeit. I. Godwin, Joscelyn. II. McLean, Adam. III. Title.
IV. Series: Magnum Opus Hermetic Sourceworks (Series) ; no. 18.
BF1623.R7R6613   1991
135'.43—dc20   91-26922
                                          CIP

Printed and bound in the United States

Contents

Introduction

The *Chemical Wedding of Christian Rosenkreutz*, often looked upon as the third Rosicrucian manifesto, has an entirely different tone from the other Rosicrucian documents and addresses itself to inner transformation rather than the outer transmutation of society and religion heralded in the *Fama* and *Confessio*. These three documents are linked together, the *Fama* being published in 1614, the *Confessio* in 1615 and the *Chemical Wedding* in 1616, comprising an orchestrated trio of publications. It seems that those who worked behind the Rosicrucian movement planned this very carefully. They first issued the *Fama*, which told of the existence of the Brotherhood. The *Confessio* followed a year later, suggesting the dawning of a new Reformation, though it also addresses some of the difficulties that the world would put in the way of such idealistic aspirations. Its tone is more guarded and realistic than that of the *Fama*, showing the Brotherhood to be aware of the forces in society that would work against their movement. Thus we have an idealistic announcement in the *Fama*, followed a year later by the more measured statement of the *Confessio*, which is capped after a further year by the publication of the *Chemical Wedding of Christian Rosenkreutz*. This elaborate Hermetic allegory certainly gave Rosicrucianism a further image, that of a group working with the alchemy of inner transformation.

Those who came upon the *Chemical Wedding* after reading the *Fama* and *Confessio* must have been quite amazed and mystified by what they read. The seeming straightforwardness of the plan of the Brethren of the Rosy Cross unfolded in the earlier documents dissolved into a mysterious convoluted allegory that few could make sense of. The *Chemical Wedding* was, however, so well-constructed and well-written that it could not merely be dismissed as nonsense. It teased the minds of those who studied it, and many tried to interpret the riddle of its allegory. It was a sensational document, a brilliant stroke of genius, for the very mystery of its elliptical allegory fired the speculation and interest of the intellectuals of Europe and ensured that Rosicrucianism would not just fade from public interest. The richness and beauty of the symbol-ism of the *Chemical Wedding* certainly gave the impression that those who had woven this marvellous allegory must possess great inner gifts.

In fact, it seems more than likely that the rumor and speculation stirred up by the *Fama* and *Confessio* would after a short time have come to nothing and faded from the public imagination without an actual appearance of the Brethren in the outer world. The *Chemical Wedding* solved this problem by showing the Fraternity of the Rosy Cross to possess a great mystery indeed, the mystery of inner transformation.

So we can see clearly just how the *Chemical Wedding* contrib-uted to the Rosicrucian phenomenon, and the extra dimension it added to the manifestos of the *Fama* and *Confessio*. It still presents itself as an allegory that can open us to the mystery of inner transformation, if we but meditate upon and immerse ourselves deeply in its symbolic substance. Although many attempts have been made to unravel its hidden meaning, few of these writers have done the work justice. The *Chemical Wedding* does not take kindly to any attempt to chisel and hack its symbols into a form reflecting the preconceived ideas of its interpreters. Anyone wishing to work with this allegory must first immerse themselves in the symbols of the story and listen inwardly to what the *Chemical Wedding* is trying to communicate. Any attempt to carve one's own path through the symbols will fail miserably, and commentators will be made to look foolish by their arrogant failure to understand and appreciate the beauty of its symbolic structure. In this sense the work seems to be esoterically protected, guarded by the depth of its mystery. Those who attempt a merely superficial interpretation, or try to shape its allegory to suit their own limited set of ideas, only reveal their own lack of insight.

The *Chemical Wedding* is thus a profound allegorical statement of the mystery of inner transformation, and the very depth of its insight shows that the Rosicrucians who worked with and created such material, must indeed have had a great degree of insight into the inner structure of the human soul.

If the Rosicrucian movement had not published the *Chemical*

Wedding and their reputation rested only upon the *Fama* and *Confessio*, history would have judged the movement merely as a publicity gimmick, a 'spoof,' or practical joke; but when one has to take the *Chemical Wedding* into account, then Rosicrucianism must be seen as possessing a deep esoteric core that one cannot dismiss lightly. Of course, one can reject the *Chemical Wedding* as being merely an interesting and well-crafted story, but anyone who honestly takes up its challenge and tries to penetrate into the profundity of its symbolism can only leave this work with a sense of the depth of its creator's esoteric insight.

The authorship of the *Chemical Wedding* has been much disputed. It is said to have been written by J. V. Andreae in 1605 when he was only nineteen, but published ten years later. However, I do not intend to here enter into a deep analysis of the controversy over its authorship.

Frances Yates in her *Rosicrucian Enlightenment* shows two possible sources in history for the symbolic material of the *Chemical Wedding*. The first was in the Garter celebrations at the court of the Duke of Württemberg at Stuttgart in 1605. Here, elaborate masques and processions were staged when the visiting English contingent of musicians and Garter Knights arrived for the ceremony of instituting Frederick of Württemberg into the Order of the Garter. The English contingent even visited the University of Tübingen where Andreae, then nineteen, was studying. The other source for the material in the *Chemical Wedding* identified by Frances Yates was the court of Frederick and Elizabeth at Heidelberg in the Palatinate from 1613 onwards. These two were sympathetic to esotericism and spiritual philosophies and gathered around them like-minded courtiers, musicians, writers, artists, and architects, who incorporated these principles into the very substance of the court. Thus the gardens at Heidelberg were laid out in an esoteric scheme with various fountains and statues, and the Elector and his Queen were especially fond of elaborate masques and processions which exhibited these spiritual principles. Frances Yates suggests that some of the scenes in the *Chemical Wedding* could indeed have been drawn from or inspired by such events at the court of Heidelberg.

Later in his life, Andreae did admit in his autobiography (*Vita ab Ipso Conscripta*) to having written the *Chemical Wedding* when a young man of nineteen, but dismissed it as a 'ludibrium' or joke of his youth. From what we know of Andreae as an orthodox and eminent Lutheran pastor and academic, it seems unlikely that he could have devised such a profoundly esoteric document, which in fact has at its basis many ideas heretical even in Protestant terms. In recent years a Lutheran apologist, J. W. Montgomery, in his book *Cross and Crucible*, tried to find a solution to this dilemma by showing the *Chemical Wedding* to be, in fact, a statement of orthodox Lutheranism. Montgomery's commentary on the *Chemical Wedding* is a perfect, though sad example of biased and blind scholarship, as he insensitively cobbles and pulverizes the text of the *Chemical Wedding* to suit his own thesis, turning the symbols upside down and inside out as his scholarly vandalism attempts to strip all the esotericism from this document. In fact, it is those very parts that he is unable to comment upon and thus ignores altogether that are perhaps the most significant from an esoteric perspective.

Andreae did write some plays in his youth which have been preserved; however, they are not on the same level as the *Chemical Wedding*. We can speculate that Andreae did in fact write a version of the *Chemical Wedding*, perhaps a simple play or masque based on or inspired by some of the Garter Celebrations he might have witnessed in 1605. Some years later during the rise of Frederick and Elizabeth in the Palatinate, one of the 'Rosicrucian' fraternity in that circle, with whom Andreae had some connections, might have decided to rework Andreae's early unpublished play into the complex esoteric allegory we know today, drawing upon the later images he was familiar with at Heidelberg. This, at least, is a view which takes into account most of the facts surrounding this document. It would be interesting if the original manuscript of Andreae's early version of the story would come to light, and this is one area where scholarly research in libraries in Germany could prove very fruitful. The Vatican may also contain some clues, as the Library of the Palatinate was plundered and partly taken to Rome at the outset of the Thirty Years War.

Although it is not possible to clear up this point of authorship with any certainty, the *Chemical Wedding* remains one of the most important Rosicrucian documents, and one which I believe contains such a depth of allegorical insight into inner transformation that it will eternally delight and challenge the human soul.

Although I have puzzled for many years over the *Chemical Wedding* since first coming across it in A. E. Waite's *Real History of the Rosicrucians*, and have many times contemplated preparing an edition of the allegory, it was a weekend study and meditation workshop at Hawkwood College at Whitsun in 1982, led by Gareth Knight, that finally impelled me to work this material into a publication. During that weekend, Gareth Knight led the company of over fifty serious students of esotericism on a guided inner journey through the symbolic landscape of the *Chemical Wedding*. The experiences of that weekend convinced me of the need to work further with this allegory, and most of the insights of my commentary have arisen out of my inner work inspired by that weekend.

It is my hope that this volume, by providing an excellent new translation by Joscelyn Godwin from the original German text, commissioned by Phanes Press, and an extensive commentary, will help those who wish to penetrate deeper into its symbols. Ultimately the *Chemical Wedding* cannot be merely understood intellectually, but must be wondered over and used as a vehicle for meditative work. I hope that some of the material presented in this book may provide the starting point for other's inner journeys, in their own exploration of the symbolic substance of this greatest of all Rosicrucian allegories.

THE
CHEMICAL WEDDING
OF
CHRISTIAN
ROSENKREUTZ

in the year 1459

"Mysteries made public become cheap
and things profaned lose their grace."

"Therefore, cast not pearls before swine
nor make a bed of roses for an ass."

"immutable knowledge"

The First Day

One evening before Easter I was sitting at table, having, as was my habit, finished my humble prayer to my Creator, and meditated on the many great mysteries which the Father of Light, in his majesty, had allowed me to glimpse. As I was trying to prepare inwardly a pure unleavened loaf to accompany my blessed Paschal Lamb, there suddenly arose such a terrific wind that I thought the mountain on which my cottage was built was going to split apart. However, I was accustomed to this kind of thing and to other tricks of the Devil, who had done me many an injury; so I took courage and remained in my meditation until, quite against expectation, someone tapped me on the back. I was so alarmed by this that I scarcely dared to turn around; yet I showed as much composure as human frailty can in such a plight. But when something pulled at my coat several times, I looked round.

There stood a wonderfully beautiful female figure, dressed all in blue, spangled like the heavens with golden stars. In her right hand she held a large trumpet all of gold, on which a name was engraved which I could plainly read, but am forbidden to reveal as yet. In her left hand she held a great bundle of letters in all languages, which, as I later learnt, she was to take to every land. She also had huge and lovely wings, studded all over with eyes, so that she could take off and fly swifter than any eagle. I might well have noticed more about her if her visit had not been so brief, and if I had not been so filled with terror and astonishment—so there I must leave it. For as soon as I turned around, she leafed here and there through her letters and at last pulled out a small note, laying it on the table with a deep curtsey and leaving me without a single word. As she flew up, she blew so loudly on her golden trumpet that the whole mountain echoed with it, and for nearly a quarter of an hour I could scarcely hear my own voice.

Poor fellow as I was, I did not know what to think or do in the face of such an unexpected encounter; so I fell on my knees and prayed my Creator not to let anything happen to imperil my eternal salvation. Then with fear and trembling I turned to the letter, which could scarcely have weighed more if it had been made from solid gold. As I examined it carefully, I found it closed with a small seal on which was engraved a delicate cross and the motto: *In hoc signo + vinces* [In this sign + you will conquer].

I was much relieved when I saw this sign, for I knew that the Devil could not stand such a seal, much less use it. So I carefully opened the letter, and found written there, with golden letters on a blue ground, the following verse:

Today—today—today
Is the wedding of the King.
If you are born for this,
Chosen by God for joy,
You may ascend the mount
Whereon three temples stand
And see the thing yourself.

Take heed,
Observe yourself!
If you're not clean enough,
The wedding can work ill.
Perjure here at your peril;
He who is light, beware!

And at the bottom it said: *Sponsus et Sponsa* [Bridegroom and Bride].

As I read this letter, I nearly fainted away, my hair stood on end, and cold sweat ran down over my whole body. Although I recognized that this was the promised wedding about which I had been told in a bodily vision seven years before, the one I had awaited so long and with such yearning, and carefully planned and calculated from my planetary tables, I would never have expected it to take place under such difficult and dangerous conditions. Originally I had thought that I would merely have to appear at the wedding to be a welcome guest; but now I was referred to divine Providence, of which up to now I was never certain.

Looking at myself, the more I pondered, I could see that there was nothing in my head but a great want of sense and a blindness in esoteric matters. And if I could not even grasp the things that lay beneath my feet, which I dealt with every day, how much less was I born for the investigation and discovery of nature's secrets! In my opinion, nature could surely have found a cleverer pupil to entrust with her precious treasure, however temporal and transient it may be.

I also found that my physical life, outward conduct, and brotherly love towards my neighbor were far from being purged and pure enough. I was aware of fleshly desires, which aim only for reputation and worldly show, not for the well-being of others; I was always thinking how I could use my skills for my own immediate benefit, for building splendid things, for making an everlasting name in the world, and other such materialistic thoughts. But what troubled me most were the dark words about the three temples, which I could not understand for all my cogitation, and would not understand even today if they had not been miraculously revealed to me.

As I trembled now in fear and hope, my thoughts straying hither and thither but especially over my weakness and incompetence, knowing no way to help myself and thoroughly unsettled by this summons, I resorted at last to my tried and trusty practice: I lay down in my bed after praying long and earnestly that my good angel might appear to me through God's grace and help me in this perplexity, as had sometimes happened before. And so it turned out, to God's glory, for my good, and for the sake of my neighbor, as a true and sincere warning and betterment.

Scarcely had I fallen asleep, when it seemed to me that I was lying in a great dark tower with countless other people, bound in heavy chains. There was no light, and we were crawling over one another like bees, thus increasing each other's suffering. Although neither I nor anyone else could see a single thing, I could hear when one person heaved himself over another, when his chains or fetters became the slightest bit lighter, although none had much to gain by this, since we were all captive wretches.

After I and the others had continued a good while in this misery, continually rebuking one another for our blindness and captivity, at last we heard the sound of many trumpets. Kettledrums rolled, too, so majestically that even in our torment we felt aroused and quickened. As the music played, the ceiling of the tower opened and a little light was let in to us. Then we could all be seen tumbling over each other in confusion, though if one person heaved himself up too high, he would fall under the others' feet. Everyone wanted to be on top, and I was no exception. Despite my heavy fetters I pressed forward with the rest and clambered up onto a stone which I had spied. Though others often grabbed at me, I defended myself with hands and feet as well as I could. We had no other thought than that we should all be set free.

But this was by no means the case. For after the authorities, who looked down on us through the gap above, had enjoyed for a while our sprawlings and moanings, a gray-haired old man ordered us to be silent, and as the noise died away began to speak, as I still remember it:

> If it would not struggle so,
> The wretched human race,
> Many a good would come to it
> From my mother's store.
> But no: since it will not obey,
> It still remains in misery
>   And must be locked up.
> Yet would my mother dear
> Not behold its sin;
> She leaves her precious gifts
> That many may see the light.
> Truly this seldom happens,
> Which makes them worth the more,
>   But this is not a fable.
> To celebrate the feast
> Which we hold today,
> To make her mercy known,
> A good work she will do.
> The rope will now come down:
> Whoever can hang on,
>   The same shall be set free.

Scarcely had he spoken these words than the old woman ordered her servants to let down the rope into the tower seven times, and to haul out those who hung onto it. Goodness! if I could only describe the excitement that seized us: everyone tried to snatch the rope, thereby hindering everyone else. But after seven minutes a sign was given by a bell, at which the servants pulled out four of us. I could not possibly reach the rope, since, as I have said, I was perched to my great distress on a stone in the wall of the tower, and hence could not touch the rope which hung down in the middle.

A second time the rope was let down. Many people's chains were too heavy, their hands too weak, so that they could not hold onto it; but as they fell they knocked down many others who might have been able to hang on. Many were actually pulled off by ones who could not reach it themselves, so that in our great distress they grew furious with one another. But those I pitied most were the ones who were so heavy that they could not rise, though their hands were torn from their bodies.

Thus it went, so that after five attempts only a few had been pulled out; for as soon as the sign was given, the servants were so quick at hauling that most people tumbled off again, and the fifth time the rope was pulled up quite empty. Hence almost everyone despaired of rescue, myself included, and cried to God to have pity on us and release us from this darkness. He must have heard some of us, for as the rope came down for the sixth time, a few hung strongly onto it. As it rose, it swung from side to side and happened, perhaps through God's will, to swing towards me. I quickly grabbed it, sat on top of all the others, and thus beyond all expectation I finally came out. Such was my joy that I took no heed of a wound in my head, caused by a sharp stone as I was pulled up, until I and the other freed prisoners had helped (as all had done before) with the seventh and last pull. Then I first realized that the effort had made my blood flow all over my clothes, having completely overlooked it in my joy.

Now after the last pull, which brought up the most people, the woman had the rope laid aside and told her exceedingly aged son (which astonished me) to tell the other prisoners their sentence. After brief consideration, he spoke up thus:

Beloved children,
Who are here,
It is fulfilled
That long was known,
Which my mother's great pity
Has bestowed on you.
You should not take it in bad part;
A blessed time will soon be yours,
When all men shall be equals,
And no one will be rich or poor.
Those to whom much was commanded
Must bring much with them.
Those entrusted with much
Will lose their skin.
So cease your great bewailing,
Which will last but a few days.

As soon as these words were spoken, the roof was replaced and locked, and the trumpets and kettledrums started up again. But loud though the music was, one could still hear the bitter laments of the prisoners coming from the tower; it soon brought the tears to my own eyes.

Thereupon the old woman sat down with her son on the seats prepared for them, and ordered for the released prisoners to be counted. When the count was done and written on a golden-yellow tablet, she asked each one's name, which was likewise written down by a pageboy. As she looked at each of us, she sighed and spoke to her son, so that I could hear: "Ah, how I sorrow for the poor people in the tower! Would God that I could free them all!" Whereupon her son answered: "Mother, it is ordered thus by God, and we must not strive against it. What if we were all lords, and possessed all the goods of earth, and were sitting at table—who would bring us our food?"

At this, the mother was silent a while, then she said: "Well, let these ones be freed from their fetters," and it was quickly done. I was almost the last, yet I could not restrain myself, though I was still watching the others, from bowing down before the old woman and thanking God, my loving father, who through her had brought me out of such darkness and into the light. Others did likewise, and the woman bowed in reply.

At last each was given a gold medal as a commemoration and as provision. One side was stamped with the rising sun; the other, as far as I remember, with these three letters: D.L.S. (*Deus Lux Solis*; *Deo Laus Semper*) [God, the light of the sun; Praise always to God]. Then each was given leave to go about his business, with the charge to serve God's glory and help our neighbor, and to guard in silence what was confided to us. This we promised, and parted from one another. But I, because of the wounds made by the fetters, found it hard going and limped with both feet. As soon as the old woman saw this, she laughed at it and called me back, saying: "My son, do not let this flaw distress you, but remember your faults and thank God that he has allowed you to attain so high a light while still in this world and in all your imperfection; and bear these wounds for my sake."

Thereupon the trumpets started up again, startling me so that I awoke. Then for the first time I realized that it had only been a dream. But it remained so strongly in my mind that I was continually troubled; it even seemed to me that I still bore the wounds on my feet. From all this I concluded that I was invited by God to attend this secret and occult wedding. Wherefore I thanked the divine Majesty with childlike trust, and prayed that he might keep me in his fear, fill my heart daily with wisdom and understanding, and at last bring me through his mercy to the desired goal, undeserving though I was.

Then I set out on my way, put on my white linen coat, and girded myself with a blood-red belt bound crosswise over my shoulders. In my hat I stuck four red roses, so that I could be more easily recognized in the crowd by this sign. For provisions I took bread, salt, and water, following the advice of one who knew, which in the event proved very fortunate. But before I stepped out of my cottage, I fell on my knees in this outfit and wedding-garment and prayed God that whatever might happen, he would bring it to a good end. Then I vowed in the sight of God that I would use everything that might be revealed to me through his grace, not for honor or prestige in the world, but only for the glory of his name and the service of my fellow men. With this vow and with high hopes I departed from my hermitage with joy.

The Second Day

As soon as I had I left my hermitage and reached the forest, it seemed to me as if the whole heavens and all the elements were already decked out for this wedding. For even the birds, I thought, sang more sweetly than usual, and the young fawns gambolled around so happily that my old heart was warmed, and, moved to song, I began to sing loudly:

Dear little bird, rejoice,
And loudly praise your maker,
Let your voice ring bright and clear;
Your God is high above.
He has prepared for you your food
And gives it in due season,
   So therefore be contented.
Why should you be sorrowful,
Why should you rail at God?
Because he's made you just a bird
Don't let it turn your head.
If he has not made you a man,
Be still: he has done well thereby,
   So therefore be contented.
How should I do, poor earthworm,
To argue with my God,
As if I had the power to fight
The very storm of heaven?
God will not be resisted thus;
Let him who thinks not so, be gone!
   Man, therefore be contented.
That he has not made you the King,
Should be no pain to you.
Perhaps you took his name in vain;
He is aware of this.
The eyes of God are sharp and keen,

He sees into your heart,
Thus God is not deceived.

I sang this song with all my heart, so that it resounded through the forest and the last words echoed back to me from the mountain, until at length I caught sight of a pleasant green meadow and stepped out of the forest. On this meadow stood three tall and splendid cedar-trees, which were so broad as to cast a lovely, welcome shadow. I was delighted by this, for although I had not come far, my great yearning was making me exhausted. So I hurried up to the trees, to rest a little beneath them.

As I approached, I perceived a tablet fastened to one of the trees. After a while I read on it the following words, written in elegant script:

Hail, guest! If you should have heard the news of the King's wedding, then hearken to these words. The Bridegroom bids us offer you the choice of four paths, by all of which you may reach the royal castle, if you do not fall by the wayside.

The first is short but perilous, and will lead you through rocky places from which you may scarcely escape.

The second is longer, and will lead you not downwards but round and round; it is flat and easy, so long as you have the aid of a magnet and do not let yourself be diverted to right or left.

The third is truly the Royal Way, which will make your journey delightful with various pleasures and spectacles. But hitherto scarcely one in a thousand has achieved it.

By the fourth way, no man may come to the kingdom, for it is a consuming path and suited only to incorruptible bodies.

Choose now which of the three you wish, and be constant thereon. But know that whichever you have taken, it is destined to you by immutable Fate, and you may go back on it only at the greatest peril of your life.

This is what we would have you know. But hearken to this warning: you do not know how much danger you incur on this way. If you are guilty of the slightest offence against the laws of our King, I beseech you to turn back while you still may, and return swiftly home by the way you came.

As soon as I had read this inscription, all my joy left me again, and I, who had been singing so cheerfully up to now, began to weep bitterly. I could see clearly the three paths before me, and knew that I would be allowed to choose one of them when the time came. But I was afraid that I would hit upon the rocky and craggy path, and fall to a miserable death. Or, if the long path were my lot, I would either lose my way or be left behind on the long journey. Of course I could not hope to be the one in a thousand who chooses the Royal Way. I could also see the fourth path before me, but it was surrounded by such fire and vapor that I dared not even venture near it. So I reflected in my mind whether I should turn back, or choose one of the paths for myself. I was painfully aware of my unworthiness, but I comforted myself with the dream in which I had been rescued from the tower. At the same time, I felt that I should not let a mere dream make me complacent; and so my thoughts went round and round, until in my great weariness my belly cried out from hunger and thirst. So I drew out my bread and cut it up.

Just then I saw a snow-white dove perched on the tree, which I had not noticed before. It fluttered down quite naturally, as perhaps it was used to doing, and approached me without fear. I gladly offered it a share of my food, which it accepted, cheering me somewhat with its beauty. But as soon as the dove's enemy, a black raven, spied it, it hurtled down upon the dove, taking no notice of me, and tried to seize its food, so that the dove's only defence lay in flight. The two birds both flew off to the South, which so angered and troubled me that I hurried thoughtlessly after the evil raven, unintentionally running nearly a field's length along one of the paths, driving off the raven and freeing the dove.

Immediately I realized how thoughtlessly I had acted: I had already taken one of the paths, and now I dared not go back on it for fear of terrible reprisals. To some extent I could put up with that, but I was most upset to have left my bag and bread behind by the tree, and to be unable to fetch them. For no sooner did I turn around than a powerful gale met me and blew me over; yet when I went forward on the path I felt nothing at all. This was enough to convince me that it would cost me my life to try to oppose the wind. So I patiently took up my cross, got to my feet, and determined to do my utmost to reach the goal before nightfall.

There appeared to be many by-ways, but thanks to my compass I avoided them. I turned not a footsbreadth from the meridian, although the path was sometimes so rough and unkept that I was quite unsure of it. On the way I thought constantly of the dove and the raven, but could not fathom their meaning. Finally I spied from a distance, on a high mountain, a splendid portal. I hastened towards this, although it lay distant and far from the path, because the sun had already sunk beneath the mountains and I could descry no other refuge. All this I attribute solely to God, who could very well have let me continue on my way, and could have shielded my eyes so that I would have missed this gate. So I hurried on, as I said, with all speed, and reached the gate while there was still daylight enough to see it.

It was an altogether fair and royal portal, carved with many wonderful images and objects, each of which, as I later discovered, had its peculiar meaning. At the top was a largish tablet with the inscription: *Procul hinc, procul ite prophani!* [Away, away from here, profane ones!], and other things which it is strictly forbidden me to tell. As soon as I stepped beneath it, out came a porter clothed in sky-blue. I gave him a friendly greeting which he returned, then he immediately demanded my letter of invitation.

Oh, how glad I was that I had brought it with me! For how easily I might have forgotten it, as had indeed happened to others, so he told me. I quickly drew it out, and he was not only satisfied but to my amazement showed me great respect, saying: "Go ahead, my brother; you are my welcome guest!" Then he asked my name, and when I answered that I was a brother of the Red Rose Cross, he was both surprised and delighted. Then he went on: "My brother, have you nothing with you to exchange for a token?" I replied that my means were scanty, but that if he liked anything that I had with me, he was welcome to it. He requested my small water-bottle, and gave me in exchange a golden token on which was nothing but the two letters: S.C. *(Sanctitate constantia; Sponsus charus; Spes charitas)* [Constant in holiness; Beloved husband; Hope, charity].

The porter asked me that if this should become useful, I would remember him. Thereupon I asked him how many had gone in before me, which he also told me. Finally he gave me, out of friendship, a sealed note for the second porter.

As I tarried a little longer with him, night fell. A great pan of pitch was lit above the gate, so that if anyone were still on the way they could hasten towards it. But the road that led on to the castle was closed in on both sides by high walls and planted with all sorts of beautiful fruit-trees. On every third tree lanterns were hung, which had been lit by a beautiful maiden, dressed likewise in blue, with a bright torch. It was so splendid and artistic to behold that I lingered more than I should have. But eventually, after I had learned enough and received useful advice from him, I took friendly leave of the first porter.

As I continued, I would have loved to know what my letter said; but since I could expect nothing unfriendly of the porter, I had to repress my curiosity and put the path behind me until I came to the second portal. This was almost identical to the first one, only with different images and decorations of mysterious meaning. The tablet attached to it read: *Date et dabitur vobis* [Give, and it shall be given to you]. Beneath this portal a frightful lion lay chained, which immediately jumped up when it saw me and came at me with a loud roar. Thereupon the second porter, who had been lying on a slab of marble, awoke and told me not to fear or fret. He drove the lion behind him and took the note, which I reached out to him with trembling hand, read it, and spoke with great reverence: "Now by God's grace is come the man whom I have long wished to see!" He also took out a token and asked me if I could redeem it. Having nothing left but my salt, I offered him that, and he accepted it with thanks. Once more, the medal bore only two letters: S.M. (*Studio merentis; Sal humor; Sponso mittendus; Sal mineralis; Sal menstrualis*) [By studying the worthy; Humor salt; Pledge for the Bridegroom; Mineral Salt; Menstrual Salt].

Just as I was trying to speak with this porter, bells began to ring from within the castle. He urged me to hurry, lest all my trouble and labor be in vain; for they were already beginning to extinguish the lights above. So quickly did I obey that in my anxiety I forgot to take leave of the porter. It was high time, for as fast as I ran, the maiden was just behind me, and all the lights were going out behind her. I could never have found my way if she had not cast some light with her torch. It was all I could do to slip in just as she did, then the door was slammed so violently that a bit of my coat was caught in it. Naturally I had to leave it behind, for neither I nor those who were already calling outside the door could persuade the guard to open it again. He swore that he had given the keys to the maiden, and that she had taken them with her into the court.

Meanwhile I looked round again at the portal. The whole world has nothing to compare with it for richness. Flanking the door were two columns: on one stood a cheerful statue with the inscription *Congratulor* [I congratulate], while the other veiled its face and looked sorrowful, and beneath it was written *Condoleo* [I condole]. In short, there were such dark and mysterious sayings and images on it, that the most learned man on earth could not have expounded them. But if God will permit, I shall soon publish and explain them all.

At this portal I had to give my name again. It was written down as the last one in a small parchment book, and delivered with others to the Lord Bridegroom. Then at last I was given the proper guest-token, a little smaller than the others, but far heavier, on which were these letters: S.P.N. (*Salus per Naturam; Sponsi praesentandus nuptiis*) [Salvation through Nature; To be presented to the Bridegroom at the wedding]. I was also given a new pair of shoes, since the floor of the castle was inlaid with pure polished marble. My old ones I was to give to one of the poor men who sat beneath the porch in great numbers, but very orderly. So I gave them to an old man.

Two pages with torches now led me to a tiny cell where they told me to sit down on a bench, which I did. They extinguished their torches in two holes in the floor, and went away leaving me sitting all alone. Soon after, I heard a noise but saw nothing: it was some men stumbling over me, but since I could not see, I had to put up with it and await what they would do. I soon realized that they were barbers, so I begged them not to push me about so: I would willingly do whatever they wanted. Thereupon they let me go, and one, whom I still could not see, cut off the hair very neatly round the top of my head, but left my long gray hair in place over my forehead, eyes, and ears. In this first encounter, I must admit, I was quite desperate, since they shoved me so hard while I was unable to see; I could only think that God was making me suffer for my curiosity. But now these invisible barbers dutifully gathered up the fallen hair and went off with it, whereupon the two pages returned and laughed heartily at me for having been so frightened.

We had scarcely exchanged a few words when someone started ringing a little bell again, which the pages told me was the signal for assembly. They invited me to follow them, and lit my way through many passages, doors, and spiral stairs, as far as a great hall. Inside was a large crowd of guests: Emperors, Kings, lords and gentlemen, noble and common, rich and poor, and all manner of people, which surprised me greatly so that I thought to myself: "Oh, what a big fool you've been, to have let yourself in for such a disagreable journey! Look: those are people you know very well and have never thought much of. They are already here, but you, for all your pleading and praying, came in last by the skin of your teeth." This and more the Devil put into my head, though I did my best to pay attention to the outcome. Meanwhile my acquaintances spoke to me, now one, now another, saying: "Well, well, Brother Rosencreutz, are you here too?"—"Indeed, my brethren," I answered, "God's grace has helped me come here, too." They found this very laughable, thinking it silly to need God's help for so slight a thing.

I had just asked one of them about his journey (for most of them had had to climb over the rocks), when some trumpets, none of which we could see, began to summon us to table. They all sat down, each one in whatever place he thought set him above the others. I and a few other poor souls were scarcely left a little room at the lowest table. The two pages entered, and one of them said such a beautiful and uplifting grace as to warm my heart. But a few louts took little notice of this, laughing and winking at each other, biting their hats, and similar fooleries. Then the food was brought in, and although not a person was to be seen, everything was managed so well that it seemed as if each guest had his own server.

As soon as my clever friends were a little refreshed, and the wine had taken away their inhibitions, the boasting began, at which they were very good. One would dare this, another that, while the most useless idiots generally bragged the loudest. When I think about the impossible and preternatural things I heard there, even today I get indignant about it. Finally they could no longer keep to their places, but one toady would be thrusting himself among the lords here, another there. They boasted of such deeds as neither Samson nor Hercules could have achieved, for all their strength. One wanted to relieve Atlas of his burden, another fetch three-headed Cerberus out of Hell again. In short, each one had his own squadron, and the great lords were so stupid as to believe their pretensions. In the end, the scoundrels got very bold, not caring though a few got their knuckles rapped with knives, and when one happened to filch a golden chain, they would all bid for it.

I saw one who could hear the sound of the heavens; another who could see the Platonic Ideas; a third would number the atoms of Democritus. Quite a few had discovered perpetual motion. Some seemed to me quite intelligent, but spoiled it by thinking too highly of themselves. Finally, there was one who would have us believe then and there that he could see the servants waiting on us, and he would have taken his insolence further, had not one of the invisible servers dealt him such a blow on his lying mouth that not only he, but many around him, fell silent as mice.

What gave me most satisfaction was that all the people I had any regard for were perfectly quiet in their conduct and made no outcry, but, aware of their lack of understanding, regarded Nature's secrets as far too high, and themselves as far too low.

In this tumult, I was close to ruing the day that had brought me here. It was painful to see how loose and wanton types sat at the table above, while I was not even left in peace in my little corner, but one of these oafs called me a fool in motley. I did not know at the time that there was still one portal to be passed, but thought that I would have to spend the whole wedding thus mocked, scorned, and humiliated. I had never done anything to deserve this, either from the Bridegroom or from his Bride; in my opinion, he should have found another fool than I to invite to his wedding. One can see from this what discontent this world's inequities can bring to simple souls. But it was actually a part of my lameness, of which

I had dreamed.

The general clamor got steadily louder. There were some who boasted of false and spurious visions, and wanted to tell us of palpably lying dreams. However, there sat near me a quiet and refined man who spoke now and then of better things. Finally he said to me: "Look, brother, if someone were to come and try to bring such hardened sinners onto the right path, do you think they would listen to him?"

"Certainly not," I replied.

"Perhaps the world wants to be deceived," said he, "and will not listen to those who wish it well. Just look at that toady: with what crazy talk and idiotic thoughts he seduces others to him! And that one there, who fools people with words of wonder and mystery. Believe me, though, the time will come when these liars will have the masks ripped from their faces, and the whole world will know what swindlers of the people lurk beneath. Then perhaps the neglected will be honored."

As he spoke thus, with the clamor becoming worse the longer it went on, there suddenly arose in the hall such a lovely and stately music as I had never heard in my life before. All fell silent in expectation of what would happen next. One could hear every stringed instrument imaginable, playing together with such harmony that I forgot myself and sat transfixed, to my neighbors' surprise. This lasted nearly half an hour, during which time none of us spoke a word; for as soon as anyone opened his mouth, something invisible gave it a blow without his knowing whence it came. I thought that since we could not see the musicians, I would have liked at least to see all the instruments on which they were playing. After half an hour, this music suddenly ceased, and we saw and heard nothing more.

Soon afterwards there arose from outside the door of the hall a great braying and rumbling of trombones, trumpets, and kettle-drums, as majestic as if the Roman Emperor himself were making his entrance. Then the door opened by itself, and the brass music grew so loud that we could scarcely bear it. At the same time there came into the hall, as it seemed to me, thousands of little lights, each moving by itself in perfect orderliness, which greatly amazed us. Finally the same two pages entered the hall with bright torches, lighting the way for a beautiful Virgin, riding on a glorious gilded triumphal throne that moved by itself. I thought that she was the same as had formerly lit and extinguished the lights, and that these were her servants whom she had placed by the trees. But now she no longer wore blue, but a shimmering snow-white garment that glittered with pure gold, and she was so bright that we could not keep our eyes on her. The two pages were almost the same, though a little less gorgeously dressed.

As soon as she reached the middle of the hall and stepped down from her seat, all the little lights bowed to her, and we rose from our benches, though each remained standing in his place. After she had shown us, and we her, all honor and reverence, she began to speak with an enchanting voice:

> The King, who is my gracious Lord,
> Is now no longer far away.
> Nor is his best beloved Bride,
> Engaged to be his wedded wife.
> Already now, with great delight,
> They've seen you all arriving here,
> And now, on every one of you
> They would bestow their favor.
> They wish most heartily that you
> May now succeed at every hour
> The coming wedding to enjoy,
> Unmixed with grief for anyone.

Here she bowed courteously again, with all her little lights, and shortly continued:

> The invitation, as you know,
> Said that none was invited here
> Who long before has not received
> The proper gifts from God, and who
> Is ignorant of how one should
>   Behave in such a place.

Therefore let none of you believe
That anyone should be so rash
To go against this hard demand;
You must imagine what it means,
If you have not been long prepared
    This wedding to attend.
Thus they remain in goodly hope
That all things will go well with you.
In these hard times, what joy it is
To see so many gathered here!
But mortals are audacious; their
Unworthiness gives them no pause;
Forward they rudely push themselves
    Where they are not invited.
That no rogue may do business here,
No knave slip in among the rest,
That all of you unhindered may
Enjoy the wedding undefiled,
Tomorrow every one of you
Upon the balance will be weighed.
Whoever is too light reveals
    What he would fain forget.
Any who, in this multitude,
Does not possess self-confidence
Will slip off quickly to the side,
For if his welcome he outstays,
All grace and favor he will lose;
Tomorrow he'll be on his way.
He whose conscience is pricking him,
May stay today within the hall,
Until tomorrow he is freed;
    Yet let him not return!
But he who knows his worthiness,
His servant will lead out of here
And show him to his chamber, where
He may retire and rest himself,
The scales awaiting happily,

Else will his sleep be hard.
The others must content themselves,
For he who dares beyond his powers
Would have done better not to come.
We wish you all the best.

As soon as she had spoken, she made another reverence and jumped gaily back onto her throne. Thereupon the trumpets began to sound again, but many of us could not suppress a deep sigh. The invisibles led her out again, but most of the little lights remained in the hall, one keeping company with each of us.

Our agitation was almost more than I can describe, and fearful thoughts and expressions were exchanged. Most people were still willing to let themselves be weighed, hoping that if they did not succeed, they might be allowed to depart in peace. I myself had thought it over briefly, and, overwhelmed by awareness of my lack of intelligence and unworthiness, I decided to remain in the hall with the others, doing better to content myself with the meal than to court a perilous failure.

After one person here, another there, had been led by his light out into a cell (each to an individual one, as I later learned), nine of us remained behind, among whom was the man I had spoken to earlier at table. Our lights did not abandon us, but after an hour one of the pages came in carrying a great bundle of cords, and asked us earnestly if we were determined to stay there. When we assented with a sigh, he bound each of us to a different place, extinguished our lights from behind, and left us wretches in the dark.

Then several of us felt the water overflowing its banks, and I myself could not restrain my tears. Although we had not been forbidden to talk to one another, pain and disappointment left us all dumb. The cord was so cunningly made that none could cut it, much less extract our feet. I took scant comfort from the thought that sore disgrace was awaiting many a one now going to his rest, whereas we could pay for our presumption in a single night. At last, in the midst of my heavy thoughts, I fell asleep. For although only a few of us closed our eyes, for sheer exhaustion I could not keep mine open.

As I slept, I had a dream, and though it may not mean much, I do not think it superfluous to tell it. I dreamed I was standing on a high mountain, and saw before me a great wide valley containing an innumerable crowd of people. Each one had a thread attached to his head, by which he was suspended from the sky. Some hung high, others low, while a number were practically standing on the ground. An aged man flew around in the air, holding in his hand a pair of shears with which he here and there snipped off a thread. Whoever hung near to earth landed the sooner, and fell without much noise. But when the turn came for a high one, he would fall so as to shake the ground. It happened to some that their threads were so stretched that they came to earth before they were cut. I much enjoyed the spectacle of this tumbling, and was heartily amused when one who had soared above his station, high in the air, crashed ignominiously and even pulled down some of his neighbors. I was just as glad when one who had kept close to earth all the time was able to land so silently that not even his neighbors noticed.

While my entertainment was at its height, one of my fellow-prisoners inadvertently jarred me, so that I awoke and was very annoyed with him. But I thought over my dream and told it to the brother who lay by me on the other side; he was quite amused, and wished that some comfort might be concealed in it. We passed the rest of the night in conversation, and impatiently awaited the coming day.

The Third Day

As soon as the lovely day had broken and the blessed sun had risen over the mountains and begun its appointed task in the high heavens, my good cohorts began to get out of bed and prepare themselves leisurely for the inquisition. One after another came back into the hall, wished us good day, and enquired how we had slept. When they saw our bonds, many of them reproached us for having been so despondent, and not, like them, unhesitatingly trusted to our luck. There were, however, a few who did not crow so loud, because their hearts were already thumping. We excused ourselves on the grounds of our lack of sense, and hoped that we would get away the quicker unharmed. We bore their mockery with the knowledge that, far from being through with the affair, they perhaps had the worst still to come.

When at length everyone was assembled again, a flourish on the trumpets and drums announced what we could only take to be the imminent arrival of the Bridegroom. But there we were wrong, for it was again the same Virgin as yesterday. She was dressed all in red velvet and girdled with a white ribbon; on her head she wore a fresh green laurel wreath, which suited her splendidly. Her train no longer consisted of little lights, but of nigh on two hundred armed men, all uniformed, like her, in red and white. As soon as she lad leaped from her seat, the Virgin came up to us prisoners, and after greeting us, said shortly:

"That some of you are aware of your wretchedness pleases greatly my severe Lord, and he wishes you to be recompensed." And when she saw me in my habit, she laughed and said:

"Are you also under the yoke? I would have thought that you were too finely turned out!"

With these words my eyes overflowed. Then she gave orders for us to be untied and coupled together, and had us placed so that we could get a good view of the scales. Then she said:

"It may go better for you than for these daredevils who are still free."

Meanwhile the scales, gilded all over, were hung up in the middle

37

of the hall, then a little table was covered with red velvet and seven weights were laid on it. First there was quite a large one, then four small ones, and lastly two more large ones. These weights were so heavy in proportion to their size that no one could believe or even imagine it. Each of the men-at-arms had, beside an unsheathed sword, a strong rope; they were grouped in seven bands corresponding to the number of weights, and in each band one man was assigned to its weight. Then the Virgin leapt back onto her high throne, and as soon as she had made her reverence, she began to speak with a loud voice;

> Whoever enters a painter's shop
> And knows not how to paint,
> And chats of it affectedly,
>   Is a laughing-stock to all.
> Whoever joins a craftsmen's guild
> And has not been elected,
> And plies the craft affectedly,
>   Is a laughing-stock to all.
> Whoever hastens to a wedding
> When no one asked him there,
> Yet enters in affectedly,
>   Is a laughing-stock to all.
> If you should climb upon this scale,
> And find you weigh too light,
> So that you fly up with a crack,
>   You're a laughing-stock to all.

No sooner had the Virgin spoken than she told one of the pages to arrange everyone according to rank and have them mount the scales one after another. One of the emperors did not hesitate, but bowed slightly to the Virgin and then climbed up in all his state apparel. Each captain laid his weight on, but to everyone's surprise the scale remained unmoved. However, the last weight was too heavy for him, and up he rose, with such disappointment that even the Virgin was sorry for him, it seemed to me. She signalled her people to hold their peace, but the good emperor was bound and delivered to the sixth band.

After him came a second emperor, climbing proudly onto the scale, for since he had a great thick book under his robe, he thought he could not fail. Scarcely was the third weight on, than he was shot up into the air so unmercifully that in his terror he let the book fall. This set all the soldiers laughing, and the emperor was handed over, bound, to the third band. So it went with quite a few emperors, who were all shamefully laughed at and put in captivity.

Next came a short little fellow, also an emperor, with a curly brown beard. After the customary bow he placed himself on the scale and stood so bravely through the weights that I thought he could even have held out for more, if there had been any. The Virgin quickly arose and went up to him, bowed, and invested him with a red velvet jacket. Then she handed to him one of the many laurel-wreaths that lay on her seat, and bade him sit down on the steps below her throne.

It would take too long to tell how it went after this with all the other emperors, kings and lords; but I cannot omit the fact that very few such noble persons were left, although many of them, contrary to my expectation, showed considerable virtues. One could withstand this weight, another that; some two, three, four, or even five; but few were able to attain final perfection. As each one proved too light, the bands of soldiers laughed heartily at him.

The testing proceeded with the noblemen, the learned men, and others, and in each class sometimes one, sometimes two, but more often not a single one was found adequate. Then came the turn of those pious gentlemen the swindlers, and the toadies who manufacture the *Lapidem spitalauficum* [Universal Cure-All]. These were put on the scale to such derision that even I, for all my sorrow, almost burst myself laughing, and the prisoners themselves could not suppress their mirth. For most of them could not even wait for the solemn sentence: they were chased from the scales with rods and scourges and led off to join the other prisoners, but each in an appropriate band. So few of the great crowd remained that I would be embarrassed to tell their number; but there were important personages among them, although everyone was honored alike with velvet clothing and a laurel-wreath.

When at last the trial was over and no one remained standing off to the side but we poor coupled hounds, one of the captains came up and spoke: "Gracious lady, if it please your grace, we would like to allow these poor people, who have acknowledged their inadequacy, to climb on the scale, too; but without any danger to them, and only in good humor. They may be some worth among them."

At first I was greatly afraid, but in my distress was comforted by the thought that in this way I would not have to be held up to derision or whipped out of the scale. I had no doubt that many of the prisoners wished they had spent ten nights with us in the hall. But since the Virgin consented, it had to be done, and so we were untied and one after the other placed on the scale. Although most failed, they were neither mocked nor beaten, but gently ushered to the side. My companion was the fifth; he held out bravely, gratifying many people, especially the captain who had put in a word for us; and the Virgin bestowed on him the customary honor. After him, two more were flipped up in the air.

I was the eighth. As soon as I stepped up, trembling, my companion looked at me encouragingly, sitting there already in his velvet, and even the Virgin smiled a little. But when I endured through all the weights, she tried to have me tugged up by main force. Yet although three men hung on to the other side of the scales, they could do nothing. Straightway one of the pages stood up and cried out as loud as he could: "It is he!" Whereupon the other answered: "Then let him have his freedom!" And this the Virgin granted.

After I had been inducted with the usual ceremony, I was given the chance of releasing a prisoner of my choice. I did not hesitate for long, but chose the first Emperor, who had pitied me from the beginning. So he was immediately set free and seated among us with all honor. Now when the last person had been weighed, but the weights proved too heavy for him, the Virgin spied the roses which I had taken from my hat and was holding in my hand. She graciously requested them of me through her page, and I willingly sent them to her. So this first act came to an end about ten o'clock in the morning, and the trumpets were sounded again. However, at the time we still could not see them.

In the meantime, the bands had to go off with their prisoners and await the sentence. Now the five chiefs and ourselves were asked our advice, and the Virgin, as President, gave each one the opportunity to voice his opinion of what should be done with the prisoners. The first suggestion was that they should all be put to death, some more harshly than others, since they had all shamelessly disobeyed the published rules. Others wanted them kept prisoner. But neither suggestion pleased the Virgin, or myself. At last the following proposal was made by the Emperor whom I had released, a nobleman, my companion, and myself: that first, all the distinguished gentlemen should be led out of the castle without delay; then others driven out more ignominiously; yet others thrown out and left to run naked; and a fourth class beaten out with rods or hunted out by hounds. Those who had voluntarily resigned the day before should be let go without any penalty; and finally, the complete rogues and those who had behaved themselves so unseemly at dinner the previous day should be corporally or capitally punished in accordance with their misdeeds.

This proposal pleased the Virgin very much, and was passed. The people were even awarded, as a bonus, a midday meal, and were immediately told of this. But the sentence would also be given at twelve o'clock noon. Here the Senate came to an end, and the Virgin went to her usual quarters with her attendants. We were assigned the highest table in the hall, with the request that we would be content with that until the whole business was finished, after which we would be led to the noble Bridegroom and Bride. To all of which we willingly consented.

Meanwhile the prisoners were brought back into the hall, and each placed according to his station. They were ordered to behave themselves somewhat better than yesterday, advice which in truth was no longer necessary, since they had completely lost heart. I can honestly state—not that I wish to flatter, but simply as a truth— that in general, the higher-class personages knew better how to conduct themselves in such unexpected misfortune. Their demeanor was poor enough, but honorable; besides, they could not yet see their keepers. But I was very glad to discover that they were now visible to us.

Although fortune had raised us so high, we still did not exalt ourselves over the others, but talked with them and urged them to be of good cheer: it would not turn out so ill. They would have liked to learn their sentences from us, but we were so strictly forbidden to tell them that we let nothing slip. Still, we comforted them as best we could, and drank with them in the hope that the wine might cheer them a little.

Our table was spread with red velvet and laid with pure silver and gold goblets, as the others noticed with astonishment and great chagrin. But before we sat down, the two pages entered and presented us all, in the Bridegroom's name, with the Golden Fleece with a flying lion. We were enjoined to wear this at table, and to guard well the honor and glory of the Order, which His Majesty thus awarded us and would soon confirm with the proper solemnity. This we accepted with the greatest humility, and promised that we would obediently discharge whatever His Majesty should desire. The noble page also had a piece of paper on which we were assigned our places in order. However, I would rather not reveal my place, so as not to be accused of pride, which is against the fourth weight.

Since we had been so magnificently treated, we asked one of the pages whether we were allowed to send some of our food down to our friends and acquaintances; and since no objection was raised, each one sent his friends a generous portion by the servants, who still remained invisible to them. Since they did not know where this was coming from, I decided to take them something myself. Scarcely had I stood up than one of the servants was upon me, saying that he wished he had politely forewarned me: for if one of the pages had seen this, and it had come to the King's ear, it would certainly have turned out badly for me. But since no one had noticed, he was not going to give me away: I, however, should henceforth pay more heed to the honor of my Order. The servant's words really terrified me, so that for a long while I scarcely dared stir in my chair. But I thanked him for his trusty warning, as well as I could in my fear and haste.

Soon the trumpets sounded again. We were quite accustomed to this by now, knowing well that it was the Virgin, so we prepared ourselves to receive her. She entered on her high throne with her usual train, one page bearing before her a tall golden goblet, another a proclamation on parchment. When she had gracefully alighted from her seat, she took the cup from the page and handed it to us in the King's name, with the news that it was sent by His Majesty, to be passed round all of us in his honor. On the lid of this cup stood Fortuna, beautifully crafted of gold, holding in her hand a flying red ensign. For this reason I drank from the cup rather less happily, being all too well acquainted with fortune's tricks.

Our Virgin was now decorated, as we were, with the Golden Fleece and the Lion, from which I observed that she was perhaps the President of the Order. We asked her what the Order's name was, but she answered that it was not time to reveal it, until after the business with the prisoners was over. For this, they were again blindfolded. What had happened to us before now seemed to them mild offence and vexation, and it was as naught in comparison to our present honor. Then she took the proclamation from the second page, divided into two parts, and something like the following was read out to the first group:

"You should confess that you have lent credence too readily to false and spurious books; that you have thought too much of yourselves, and entered this castle to which no one invited you. If perhaps the majority of you simply wanted to slip in here in order to live more grandly and pleasurably, you have egged one another on to such outrage and effrontery that you have well deserved to suffer condign punishment."

They humbly acknowledged it and raised their hands. Then the other group were addressed more harshly in the following terms:

"You know very well, and stand convicted by your consciences, that you have forged false and spurious books, fooled and swindled others, thereby lowering the royal dignity in everyone's eyes. You also know what blasphemous and seductive pictures you have used, sparing not even the Holy Trinity, but using it for the cozening of one and all. Now it has come to light what tricks you have played on the rightful guests, and how you have introduced unsuspecting ones. Everyone knows that that you have been involved in open whoring, adultery, debauchery, and every kind of uncleanness, all of it in defiance of the well-known law of our kingdom. In short, you know that you have demeaned His Majesty before the common people; wherefore you should admit that you are publicly convicted swindlers, toadies, and scoundrels, who deserve to be sundered from decent folk and severely punished."

The worthy artists were extremely reluctant to confess to all this. Not only did the Virgin threaten them, on her oath, with death, but the other group shouted loudly against them and complained with one voice that they had been deceitfully seduced by them. In the end, for fear of a still worse fate, they sorrowfully confessed their guilt. But they proposed, in mitigation, that they alone should not be blamed so harshly for what had happened. For when the noblemen were wanting to gain admission to the castle and were laying out great sums of money, each man had used his wits to get some; and so it had come to the present pass, as all could see. Since it had miscarried, in their opinion they deserved no more punishment than the nobles. The latter should surely have had the good judgment to see that one who was certain of getting in would not for mere gain, and in such danger, have clambered over the wall with them. Their books, moreover, had sold so well that anyone who could not live by other means was compelled to practice such a fraud. Therefore they hoped that if justice was to be done, no harm would come to them, since they had behaved as servants should towards their lords, upon the latters' earnest entreaty.

With such arguments they tried to excuse themselves. But they were answered thus: "His Majesty has decided to punish one and all, some more severely, others less so. What you have proposed is indeed partly true, and on that account the nobles will not be entirely acquitted. Those, however, who have acted out of malice or corrupted the ignorant against their will, should prepare to die. Likewise those who have uttered false libels against His Majesty, as all can see from their own writings and books."

Thereupon arose a pitiful weeping and wailing, pleading and prostration, but it was to no avail. I was amazed at how the Virgin stood unmoved by their misery, whereas even we, to many of whom they had caused much suffering and anguish, were moved to pity and tears. Quickly she sent her page, who brought back with him all the men-at-arms who had attended the weighing earlier today. They were then ordered each to take his own band and lead them out in orderly procession to the great garden, every prisoner attended by a cuirassier. It astonished me to see how accurately each soldier recognized his own. But my companions of yesterday were permitted to go freely into the garden and witness the execution of the verdict.

As soon as all were outside, the Virgin leaped onto her throne and bade us sit down on the steps and attend the execution. We did as we were told, leaving everything on the table except the goblet, which the Virgin committed to the page's keeping, and, wearing our decorations, mounted the throne. It slid forward by its own power as gently as if it had been floating in the air, and thus we came to the garden where we all dismounted.

This garden was not particularly ornamental, but I was delighted by the way the trees were set out in rank and file. A fine fountain was also running there, decorated with wonderful pictures and inscriptions, also with strange symbols (which, God willing, I will explain in a future book). A wooden structure was erected in this garden, hung with beautiful painted cloths. It had four galleries, one above the other. The first was the most lordly, hence was hung with a white satin curtain so that we could not tell who was behind. The second was empty and undecorated. The last two were hung with red and blue satin.

As we neared the scaffold, the Virgin bowed almost to the ground, filling us with fear, for we could easily tell that the King and Queen must not be far off. As soon as we too had made obeisance, the Virgin led us by the spiral stair to the second gallery. There she placed herself at the head, and us in the same order as before. For fear of malicious gossip, I cannot now tell how the Emperor whom I had rescued conducted himself towards me, as he had done earlier at table. For he could well see what distress and misery he would now have been in without me, awaiting his sentence in shame, and how, thanks to me, he now stood there in such dignity and honor. Meanwhile, the maiden who had originally brought me the invitation, and whom I had never seen again, stood forth, blew one blast on her trumpet, and with a loud voice pronounced the sentence:

"His Majesty informs all gentlemen present of his sincere wish that one and all assembled here had appeared at his invitation, with such qualities that they might honor him by attending the wedding banquet. But since it has otherwise pleased Almighty God, His Majesty will not complain, but must reluctantly abide by the ancient and laudable usage of this kingdom. However, that His Majesty's innate kindness may be celebrated throughout the world, he has decreed, with his advisors and representatives, that the usual sentence should be considerably mitigated.

"Therefore, in the first place, all noblemen and rulers shall not only have their lives spared, but shall straightway be set free to depart. He asks that your good Lordships be not vexed that you cannot be present at His Majesty's wedding, but reflect that if Almighty God has given you a burden that you cannot easily and patiently bear, he also has an unfathomable wisdom in the distribution of talents. Therefore it shall be no disgrace to your Lordships' reputation to be excluded from such an Order as ours; for we cannot all attain all things.

"Since your Lordships have been misled by evil toadies, these shall not go unpunished. Next, His Majesty wishes to share with you a catalogue of heretical writings, or an *Index expurgatorium* [Index of things to be purged], whereby you may more wisely sift the good from the bad. And since His Majesty intends before long to overhaul his own library and sacrifice the offending books to Vulcan, he requests your friendship, service, and grace, that each may do likewise with his own, so that hopefully in the future all this evil and rubbish shall be destroyed. Moreover, may you be warned hereby never again to demand admittance here, lest your excuse about seducers be withdrawn and you suffer the contempt and mockery of all. Lastly, since the province has something to demand from your lordships, let none demur to ransom himself with a chain, or whatever he has to hand, and thus depart from us in friendship, and under our escort make his way back to his own.

"The others, however, who did not resist the first, third, and fourth weights, are not so lightly dismissed by His Majesty. That they may also feel his mercy, his command is that they be stripped entirely naked and thus sent away.

"Those who were proved too light by the second and fifth weight shall be stripped and then branded with one, two, or more marks according to each one's offence.

"Those who were raised up only by the sixth or seventh weight shall be treated somewhat more mercifully..." (And so forth, a specific punishment being set for each combination, which would take too long to enumerate here.)

"Those who voluntarily resigned yesterday shall be allowed to go free from all obligation.

"Lastly, the arrant swindlers who could not even outweigh a single weight shall suffer capital or corporal punishment according to their deserts, with the sword, the rope, with water, or with rods. And this sentence shall be executed strictly as an example to all."

Thereupon our Virgin broke her staff in two. The other maiden, who had read the sentence, sounded her trumpet and with a deep obeisance went to those standing behind the curtain.

I cannot forbear here from telling the reader something of the number of our prisoners. Those who equalled one weight were seven; two weights: twenty-one; three weights: thirty-five; four weights: also thirty-five; five weights: twenty-one; six weights: seven. One was raised only with difficulty by all seven weights, and this was the one I had redeemed. Those who failed to raise any weight at all were many; and, lastly, those who raised them all from the ground were few. So I counted them carefully and noted them on my writing-tablet, as they stood distinctly before us. It seemed remarkable to me that among all those who weighed anything, no two were exactly the same. For although, as I said, thirty-five of them equalled three weights, in one case it would be the first, second and third; in another the third, fourth, and fifth; in another, the fifth, sixth, and seventh, and so forth. Thus, amazingly enough, among all the hundred and twenty-six who weighed anything, no two were the same. If time would permit, I would name them all with their respective weights; but I hope it may be published in the future with the interpretation.

Now as this sentence was read out, the nobles were at first quite happy, since in the face of such severity they had not reckoned on getting a light sentence. Thus they gave more than was demanded, each paying with whatever chains, metalwork, gold, money, etc., he had about him, and politely taking his leave. Although the royal servants were forbidden to jeer at them as they went, a few jokers could not keep from giggling; for it was comical enough to see how fast they made their escape without a backward glance. A few asked that the promised catalogue might be sent them at once, for they wanted to deal with their books as would please His Majesty. This was also promised them. Beneath the porch each was given a beaker of *Oblivionis haustus* [the draught of forgetfulness], so that he might forget his misfortune.

After these, the volunteers departed; they were allowed to go because of their good sense, but never again might they return in the same condition. However, if they, like the others, should receive further revelations, they would be welcome guests.

Meanwhile the culprits were being stripped, and here too appropriate distinctions were made. Some were driven away naked but unmolested; some were decked out with bells and jingles; some pursued with whips. In short, the penalties were so various that I cannot enumerate them all. Finally it came to the last ones, whose treatment took a little longer; for it took a considerable time for some to be hanged, some beheaded or drowned, and others put to death in different ways. My eyes truly ran over at this execution, not so much because of the punishments which they had well deserved for their crimes, but in reflection on human delusion, in that we are always meddling in that which has been sealed up for us since the Fall of Man.

Now the garden, formerly so crowded with people, was almost empty, and none but the men-at-arms remained. When all was over, there was silence for five minutes. Then there came a beautiful, snow-white unicorn with a golden collar on which were certain letters; it stepped up to the fountain and knelt down on its forelegs, as if it wished to honor the lion which stood upon the fountain, so still that I had taken it for stone or bronze. Immediately the lion took the naked sword that it held in its claws, and broke it in two in the middle, whereupon the pieces appeared to me to sink in the water. Then it roared long, until a white dove flew up, bringing in its little beak a sprig of olive which the lion straightway swallowed and was satisfied. The unicorn also returned contentedly to its place.

Hereupon our Virgin again descended the spiral stair from the wooden structure, and we made our obeisance towards the curtain. Then we had to wash our hands and heads in the fountain, and wait a little while in our order until the King had returned to his hall through a concealed passageway. We were conducted out of the garden and back to our former quarters with special music, in great pomp and splendor, and with elevated conversation. This was toward four o'clock in the afternoon.

In order to make the time pass more quickly, the Virgin had appointed each of us a well-bred page, not only richly dressed but also well educated. These pages could discourse on any subject so knowingly that we were quite put to shame. They had the duty of showing us around the castle, though not everywhere, so as to pass the time and satisfy our curiosity. Meanwhile the Virgin took her leave, promising us that she would reappear at supper and then celebrate the ceremony of *suspensionis ponderum* [the hanging of the weights]. She bade us await the next day with patience, for then we must be presented to the King.

When she had taken leave of us, each one did as he pleased. Some looked at the beautiful pictures that were shown to them, and were curious to know what the mysterious symbols might mean. Others needed to refresh themselves again with food and drink. But I let myself be guided round the palace by my page, together with my companion, and will never regret that tour as long as I live; for among many wonderful antiquities I was also shown the Tombs of the Kings, where I learned more than is to be found in all the books in the world. There, too, stands the miraculous Phoenix, about which I published a special booklet two years ago. (I also intend, if my narrative should prove fruitful, to publish separate treatises on Lions, Eagles, Gryphons, Falcons, and other things, with their illustrations and inscriptions.) I am only sorry that my other companions missed such treasures; yet I suppose this must have been God's express desire. I was especially glad of my page, for according to each person's interest, his page led him into the places and situations that he would enjoy. Mine alone was entrusted with the keys to this place, because this pleasure was reserved especially for me. Others, indeed, were invited, but they thought that such tombs would only be found in the churchyard, to which they would come soon enough if there were anything worth seeing there. But I would not withold from my grateful students the tombs that the two of us drew and transcribed.

The other thing shown to us both was the marvelous library. Everything was there, complete, as before the Reformation. But even though my heart leaps whenever I think of it, I will not yet tell about it, because its catalogue is shortly to be published. By the entrance to this room stood an enormous book such as I had never seen, in which were pictured all the figures, chambers, portals, all the inscriptions, riddles, and suchlike, to be seen in the whole castle. Although I have also promised to give some of these, it seems not yet the proper time; I must first learn to know the world better. In every book the author's portrait was painted. Many of these, as I understood, were to be burnt, so that their memory would be blotted out among righteous men.

When we had perused these things and had just left, another page ran up to us and whispered something into our page's ear. The latter gave up the keys to him, which the other immediately took up the spiral staircase. Our page had turned as white as death, and when we beset him with questions, he informed us that His Majesty wanted no one to visit either the Library or the Tombs; hence he begged us, for his life's sake, not to give him away to anyone, since he had just denied it. This we also promised him, half in joy and half in fear, and fortunately it remained secret, for no one asked us any more about it. We had spent three hours in the two places, which I will never regret.

Although it had already struck seven, we had still been given nothing to eat; but our hunger was easily satisfied by the continual stimulation, and I could have fasted my life long on nourishment like this. We were also shown ingenious waterworks, mines, and various ateliers, none of which failed to surpass all of our arts and crafts taken together. The rooms were all arranged in a semicircle, so that they had a view of the splendid mechanical clock mounted on a beautiful tower in the center, and could regulate themselves according to the movements of the planets which were charmingly depicted on it. There again it was clear to me how far short our own artists fall, although it is not my business to instruct them.

At length we came to a large hall which the others had been shown long before. In the middle stood a terrestrial globe thirty feet in diameter, although nearly half of it, except a little that was covered by the steps, was sunk in the ground. Two men could easily turn this globe and its apparatus, so that the same amount was always visible above the horizon. Although I could well see that this instrument had some particular purpose, I could not understand what was served by the small golden circles visible at various places on it. My page laughed at this and told me to examine them more closely. I found thereon my own country, also marked with gold, whereupon my companion searched for his own and found it likewise. Since this was also the case with the other bystanders, the page assured us that yesterday the old astronomer Atlas had shown His Majesty that the gilded points indicated with perfect accuracy the homes of all the elect. For this reason the page, too, when he saw that I had excluded myself, although there was a mark on my country, had instructed one of the captains to plead for us, that we might take our chances on the scales without risk, especially since the country of one of us had a remarkably favorable sign. Hence also he, who of all the pages had the most influence, had not been assigned to me without reason. I thanked him for this and looked more carefully at my native land, noticing that near the circle were some delicate rays (though I do not mention this for my own name and fame). I saw much more on this globe that I prefer not to reveal; everyone may ask himself why every town does not have its philosopher.

After this he led us right into the globe, which was made so that on the sea, where there was otherwise a great empty space, there was placed a tablet with three dedications and the artist's name; one could raise this gently, and gain access via a slender bridge to the center, where there was room for four people. Nothing else was inside but a round bench on which we sat, and even in full daylight (it was now dark) could contemplate the stars. I think these were made from pure carbuncles, glittering so beautifully in their proper order and courses that I could scarcely bear to leave, as the page later told our Virgin, for which she often teased me. For it was already mealtime, and I had stared so long inside the globe that I was almost the last at table.

I could tarry no longer, and as soon as I had put on my coat, which I had laid aside, I came to the table. The servants greeted me with such bowing and scraping that I dared not look up for shame, and thus accidentally left the Virgin standing as she awaited me to one side. As soon as she noticed, she pulled me by the gown and led me to table. I need tell no more about the music and other delights, partly because I am quite unworthy to describe them, and partly because I have already done so as best I can. In a word, there was nothing but artistry and beauty. After we had told each other of our various experiences of the afternoon (though the Library and the Tombs were not mentioned), and were feeling merry from the wine, the Virgin began to speak:

"Gentlemen, I am having a great argument with one of my sisters. In our room we have an eagle whom we are both feeding with meat in order to win his affection, and this has caused much ill-will. One day we decided to go to him together, and let him belong to whichever of us he was most friendly to. We did so, with myself, as usual, carrying a branch of laurel in my hand. When the eagle saw us both, he quickly gave my sister a twig that he had in his beak, and then begged for mine, which I gave him. Now each one believes that he likes her best. What should I do about this?"

We all enjoyed the Virgin's modest proposal, and everyone would gladly have heard the solution; but since all their eyes rested on me, and they wanted me to begin, I was so muddled in my head that I could do nothing but ask another riddle. So I said: "Gracious Lady, it would be easy to answer your question if it were not for a trouble of my own. I had two friends, both extraordinarily attached to me. Since they could not decide which of them loved me the most, they made up their minds to run up to me unawares. Whoever I embraced first, he would be the one. This they did, but since one could not keep up with the other, he was left behind and wept. I received the other with surprise. When they explained the trick, I knew no way out, and so I have been stuck to this day, in the hope of finding good counsel here."

The Virgin thought this over, well seeing what I was about, and therefore answered: "Very good, then let us two be quits! Let the others propose a solution!"

But I had already made them wise, and so a second one began: "In my town a maiden was lately condemned to death. But the judge was so sorry that he let it be known that if anyone would fight for her, she should be his. Now she had two lovers. One immediately came to the lists to await his adversary. Then the other also presented himself, but since he came too late, he decided all the same to fight for her, and willingly let himself be beaten, so that her life would be spared. And this he did. Afterwards both of them wanted her. Now tell me, gentlemen, which of the two had won her?"

Then the Virgin could hold back no longer, and said: "I hoped to learn much, but now I am ensnared myself. Still, I would like to hear if anyone else has something to say."

"Indeed," answered a third, "never has a stranger story been told than what once happened to me. In my youth I was in love with a virtuous girl. In order to bring my love to its desired goal, I employed an old woman who would take me with her to visit the girl. Now it happened that the girl's brothers came upon us while the three of us were alone together. They were so angry that they wanted to kill me, but I implored them so much that they finally made me swear to take each one to wife for a year. Now tell me, gentlemen: should I have taken the older or the younger one first?"

We all laughed heartily at this riddle, and although some whispered together, none wanted to make the choice.

Then a fourth began: "There lived in a town an honorable, aristocratic lady whom many admired, but especially a young nobleman. He became so importunate that she finally gave him this ultimatum: he could have his way if, in the middle of winter, he could lead her into a beautiful green rose-garden; if not, then he could never see her again. Thereupon the nobleman traveled in every land to find a man who could bring this about, until at last he came upon an old fellow who promised to do it on condition that he would give him the half of his possessions. He agreed, and the other arranged it. He invited the woman to his garden, and to her astonishment she found everything green, pleasant, and warm.

When she remembered her vow, she asked to go once more to her husband, to whom she poured out her sorrow with sighs and tears. He, however, knowing well her faithfulness, sent her back to her lover who had bought her so dear, to redeem her promise. The nobleman was so moved by the husband's integrity that he felt it would be sinful to touch so virtuous a wife, and sent her back honorably to her husband. Now, when the little old man learnt of their fidelity, poor as he was, he did not want to be left out; so he gave the nobleman back all his property, and departed. Now, gentlemen, I do not know which of these people displayed the greatest virtue."

This tale left us all speechless; even the Virgin had no answer but to ask another of us to go on. So the fifth began without delay: "Gentlemen, I will make it short. Who has the greater joy: the one who beholds his beloved, or the one who only has her in his thoughts?" "The one who sees her," said the Virgin. "No," I replied, whereupon an argument began. Then the sixth cried out: "Gentlemen, I would take a wife; but I have the choice of a maiden, a married woman, and a widow. Help me out of my dilemma, and I will help you settle yours."

"Nothing easier," replied the seventh, "if the choice is free. But for me things are different. In my youth I loved a beautiful, virtuous girl from the bottom of my heart, and she loved me, but her kinsman would not give permission for us to marry. So she was married to another man, honest and upright, who kept her with modesty and affection until she came to childbed, and was so ill that everyone thought she had died. With great sorrow, they gave her a magnificent burial. Then I thought to myself: if this person could not be yours in life, at least you can embrace her in death and kiss her to your heart's content. So I took my servant with me, and dug her up again by night. When I opened the coffin and took her in my arms, I felt her heart and discovered that it was still beating a little. As I warmed her it became stronger and stronger, until I could see that she was indeed still alive. Then I silently took her home with me and, after warming her frozen body with a bath of precious herbs, committed her to the care of my mother until she gave birth to a fine son, whom I had cared for as lovingly as I had the mother. After two days, since she was greatly confused, I revealed to her all that had occurred, and asked her to live as my wife from now on. But she was greatly worried that it might give grief to her husband, who had treated her well and honorably. However, as such things will turn out, she now felt no less obligated to one as to the other.

"After two months, being then obliged to travel elsewhere, I invited her husband as a guest and asked him among other things whether he would take back his dead wife, if she were to come home again. He affirmed it with tears and lamentations. Finally I brought his wife to him, together with her son, told him all that had happened, and asked him to give consent for my intended marriage. After a long argument he could not shake my claim, and so had to leave the wife with me. Then came the battle over the son..."

The Virgin here interrupted him and said: "I am surprised that you could thus increase the poor man's misery."

"What?" he answered, "Was I not concerned about it?"

Thereupon an argument arose among us, in which most of us were of the opinion that he had done right. But he said: "Not at all: I gave him back both wife and son! Now tell me, gentlemen, which was the greater: my integrity or this man's happiness?"

These words had so aroused the Virgin that she straightway had a toast sent round in honor of these two. Then followed the stories of the others; but since they were somewhat confused, I cannot recall them all. Only one still occurs to me. He said that a few years ago he knew a physician who had bought wood against the winter, and the whole winter long had kept himself warm with it. But when spring approached, he sold the same wood again and thus warmed himself for nothing. "That must be an art!" said the Virgin, "But it is too late for it today." "Yes," answered my companion, "whoever cannot solve all the riddles may ask for the answers by messenger; this, I think, cannot be refused."

Now grace was said, and we all stood up from the table, more satisfied and merry than glutted: I could wish that all feasts and meals were conducted thus. As we were taking a turn or two in the hall, the Virgin asked us whether we would like to make a start with the wedding. "Gladly," said one, "O noble and virtuous maiden!"

Thereupon she discreetly sent a page off, but continued in conversation with us. She was so familiar with us that I was bold enough to ask her name. Then the Virgin smiled at my impertinence, but did not get annoyed, and answered:

"My name contains five-and-fifty, and has but eight letters. The third is the third part of the fifth; if it is added to the sixth, they make a number whose root exceeds the first letter by as much as the third itself, and is half of the fourth. The fifth and seventh are equal, and the last is equal to the first, and these make as much with the second as the sixth, which is just four more than thrice the third. Now tell me, Sir, what is my name?"

The riddle seemed thorny enough. However, I did not give up, but asked: "Noble and virtuous maiden, might I not know a single letter?" "Yes," she said, "that would be all right." "Then how much," I went on, "would the seventh be worth?" "It is as many as the gentlemen here." Then I was satisfied, and easily worked out her name. This pleased her, and she said that more would be revealed to us soon.

In the meantime, a number of maidens had made themselves ready and now entered with great show. Before them two youths lighted the way; one had a cheerful face, bright eyes, and a fine figure, but the other looked somewhat petulant: whatever he wanted, must be done, as I afterwards learnt. Next followed four maidens: one of them very demure in her conduct, looking modestly at the ground; the second equally modest and bashful; the third was frightened of something as she entered the room. As I understood it, she cannot long remain where people are too hearty. The fourth carried some bouquets to indicate her friendliness and generosity.

After these four maidens came two others, more elaborately dressed, and greeted us courteously. One wore a deep blue dress set with little golden stars; the other was all in green, ornamented with red and white stripes. Both had loose kerchiefs on their heads which looked utterly charming. Lastly came one on her own who wore a coronet on her head, and looked up to heaven rather than to earth. We all thought she must be the Bride, but were far wrong, although she so outdid the Bride in nobility, wealth, and status that she afterwards dominated the whole wedding-feast.

At this point we all followed the example of our Virgin, sinking deep on our knees, although the lady behaved very humbly and reverently. She offered each her hand, and bade us not to be too surprised at this, for it was the least of her gifts. But we should lift our eyes to our Creator and learn to recognize his omnipotence here, then lead our lives as before, using this grace for the glory of God and the good of mankind. Her words were very different from those of our Virgin, who was somewhat more worldly; they pierced through my very marrow. "And you," she went on, addressing me, "have received more than others; see that you also give more!" This sermon puzzled me greatly.

When we noticed the maidens with instruments, we thought we were going to have to dance, but the time had not yet come. The weights, about which I have told, were still all there. Hence the Queen (though I still did not know who she was) told each maiden to take one of them. She gave her own, the last and biggest, to our Virgin and bade us follow her. Now our prestige was somewhat lessened, and I was well aware that our Virgin had been overkind to us, and that we were not valued as highly as we had sometimes begun to imagine. So we went out in our usual order until we reached the first room, where our Virgin was the first to hang up the Queen's weight. Then a beautiful anthem was sung.

In this room was nothing valuable but some fine little prayerbooks, such as one should never be without. In the middle stood a tall lectern, excellently suited for prayer. The Queen knelt down at this, and we all had to kneel around her and pray after her as she read from one of the books, namely that the wedding might go forward to God's glory and to our benefit. Then we moved to the second room, where the first maiden hung up her weight, and so forth until the ceremony was completed. Thereupon the Queen again gave each her hand and took her leave with her maidens.

Our President stayed with us a while, but since it was already two o'clock in the morning, she did not want to keep us longer. It was my impression that she enjoyed being with us. She wished us a good night and a peaceful sleep, but it seemed as if she parted from us

unwillingly. Our pages knew their business well; they showed each
to his bedroom and remained with us in another bed, so as to be at
hand if we should need anything. My bedroom (I know nothing of
the others) was royally furnished and hung with beautiful tapestries
and paintings. Most of all I liked my page: he was so well informed
and accomplished that he kept me up for yet another hour, and I did
not fall asleep until half past three.

That was the first night I went to sleep in peace. Nevertheless, a
dreadful dream kept me from being too contented: all night long I
was struggling with a door I could not open. Finally I succeeded, and
in such fantasies passed the time until, towards dawn, I awoke.

The Fourth Day

I was still lying in my bed, calmly looking at the wonderful pictures and sculptures that filled my room, when suddenly I heard cornets playing, as if the procession had already started. My page jumped out of bed like a mad thing, looking more dead than alive; and you can imagine how I felt, too, when he said that the others were already being presented to the King. I did not know what to do, beyond weeping bitterly and bemoaning my laziness, but I got dressed. My page was ready much sooner and ran out of the room to see how things stood. Soon he returned, bringing the welcome news that nothing was lost: I had merely slept through breakfast, and they had not had me woken on account of my age. But now it was time to go with him to the fountain, where most of them were assembled.

My spirits rose on hearing this, and I was soon ready in my outfit. I followed the page to the fountain in the same garden as yesterday. When we had greeted one another, and the Virgin had teased me for a slug-a-bed, she led me by the hand to the fountain. Here I found that the lion, instead of his sword, had a largish tablet, which on closer examination I found to be taken from the ancient monuments and put here in the place of honor. The writing had deteriorated from age, but all the same I will give it here for anyone to meditate on:

HERMES PRINCEPS.
POST TOT ILLATA
GENERI HUMANO DAMNA,
DEI CONSILIO:
ARTISQUE ADMINICULO,
MEDICINA SALUBRIS FACTUS
HEIC FLUO.
Bibat ex me qui potest: lavet, qui vult:
turbet qui audet:
BIBITE FRATRES, ET VIVITE.

∞ ꙮ꙳꙳ XXꙨIC ꙮꙮꙮ꙳

[Prince Hermes. After so many injuries done to the human race, by God's counsel, and by the aid of art, here I flow, made a healing medicine. Drink from me who can; wash who wishes; stir who dares; drink, brethren, and live.]

This writing was simple to read and understand, so it can well be given here, being easier than the rest. After we had begun by washing in the fountain, each took a drink from a solid gold beaker. Then we had to follow the Virgin once more into the hall, and there don new clothes of cloth-of-gold, beautifully decorated with flowers. Each one was given a second Golden Fleece, set with precious stones and each worked according to the individual craftsman's skill. On it hung a heavy piece of gold picturing the sun and moon opposite one another. On the reverse was this saying: "The moon's light shall be like the sun's light, and the sun's light shall be seven times as bright." Our previous decorations were put in a case and entrusted to one of the servants.

After this the Virgin led us in order outside, where the musicians were already waiting by the door, all dressed in red velvet with white borders. Thereupon a door, which I had never seen open before, was opened to the royal staircase. The Virgin led us and the musicians up its 365 spiral steps. Here we saw nothing but fine and precious workmanship; the higher we went, the more splendid the decorations became. At length we came out at the top into a painted vault, where sixty maidens were awaiting us, all daintily dressed. They bowed to us, and we made our reverence to them as best we could, then our musicians were sent back down the stairs and the door was shut. A little bell was rung, whereupon a beautiful maiden entered, bringing each one a laurel-wreath; but our maidens were given branches.

Then a curtain was drawn back, and I saw the King and Queen sitting there in their majesty. And if yesterday's Queen had not been so kind as to warn me, I would have forgotten myself and compared such unspeakable splendor to Heaven itself: for though the room shone with pure gold and precious stones, the Queen's robes were such that I could not look on them. It was as far above what I had formerly thought beautiful as the stars in the sky. Now the Virgin came in, and taking each of the maidens by the hand presented her with a deep bow to the King. Then the Virgin spoke:

"May it please Your Majesties, gracious King and Queen: the gentlemen here present have come at the risk of life and limb. Your Majesties have reason to rejoice, since the majority are well qualified to contribute to Your Majesties' kingdom and estates, as will be ascertained from each one. I therefore pray to present them humbly to Your Majesties, and humbly beg to be discharged of this my commission, and that each be questioned graciously about my deeds and omissions."

Thereupon she laid her laurel-branch on the ground. It would have been fitting now if one of us had said a few words, but we were all tongue-tied. At last the aged Atlas came and spoke on the King's behalf: "Their Majesties are well pleased by your arrival, and wish one and all to receive the royal favor. They are well satisfied with your conduct, dear maiden, on which account a royal honor will be reserved for you. But they think that you should continue to attend them today, as they have nothing with which to reproach you." The Virgin therefore took up her branch again, and for the first time we had to step aside with her.

The front of this chamber was rectangular, five times as long as it was broad, but towards the exit it had a great apse like a portal in which stood in a circle three royal thrones, the middle one somewhat higher than the others. Two people sat on each throne. On the first was an old king with a grey beard, but his consort was very beautiful and young. On the third throne sat a black king of middle age, and beside him a dainty old matron, not crowned but wearing a veil. On the middle throne sat two young persons with laurel-wreaths on their heads, while over them hung a great ornamental crown. They were not as attractive as I had imagined them, but so it must be. Behind them on a round bench sat a number of old men, none of whom, to my surprise, wore a sword or any other weapon; I also saw no bodyguards. The maidens who had been with us yesterday were sitting in a curve by the side.

Here I must mention something else. Little Cupid flew around, especially flitting playfully around the great crown. Sometimes he went in between the lovers and teased them with his bow, and now and then he even seemed about to shoot one of us. In short, the child was so mischievous that he would not even leave the little birds alone that flew in great numbers around the chamber, but annoyed them whenever he could. The maidens had a short way with him, and when they caught him he could not easily escape. This little knave provided great diversion and amusement.

Before the Queen stood an altar, small but exquisitely decorated, on which were a black velvet book discreetly overlaid with gold, and beside it a small taper in an ivory candlestick. For all its smallness it burned on and on, and if Cupid had not sometimes blown on it for fun, we would not have taken it for a fire. Near this stood a sphere or celestial globe, turning neatly on its own; also a little striking clock; and next a tiny crystal fountain out of which a clear blood-red liquid continually ran; and lastly a skull in which was a white snake, so long that although it crawled round and encircled all the objects, its tail remained in one of the eyeholes of the skull until its head came back to the other, so that it never left its skull. But if Cupid tweaked it a little, it instantly vanished inside, leaving us all astounded.

Besides this altar, there were here and there in the chamber wonderful images which all moved as if they were alive, and were full of such fantasy that I cannot possibly describe them all. As we left the room, there arose an extraordinary music of voices, of which I could not say whether it came from the maidens who were still inside, or from the images themselves.

Being now well satisfied, we exited with our maidens and found our musicians all ready to conduct us down the spiral staircase; but the door was carefully locked and bolted. As soon as we were back in the hall, one of the maidens began: "Sister, I was surprised that you dared go among so many people." "My sister," answered our President, "None of them worried me so much as this one!" and she pointed to me. This speech hurt my feelings, for I could well see that she was mocking my old age. And indeed, I was the oldest of all. Then she comforted me again with the assurance that if I would behave myself with her, she would certainly relieve me of this burden.

Now the meal was brought in and each sat beside his maiden. They well knew how to make the time fly with charming conversation, but I must not chatter about their gossip and games out of school. Most of the talk was about the arts, by which I learnt soon enough that young and old were well acquainted with them. But I was still thinking about how I might make myself young again, and this made me sad.

The Virgin, seeing this, said: "I know what this young fellow needs: if I were to sleep with him the coming night, he would be happier in the morning." Then they started to laugh, and although I blushed from head to toe, I had to laugh at my own misfortune. There was one who tried to turn my shame back on the Virgin, saying: "I hope that not only we but the maidens themselves will bear witness to our brother that our Virgin President has promised to sleep with him tonight." "I should be happy at that," answered the Virgin, "if I had not my own sisters here to fear; for what would they do if I were to choose the fairest and best without their leave?" "My sister," began another, "we can see from this that your high office has not made you proud. If by your permission we may make these gentlemen our bedfellows, choosing them by lot, we are most happy for you to exercise your prerogative."

We left it at that, thinking it a joke, and began to talk to each other again; but our Virgin would not leave us in peace, and began again: "Sirs, what if we let chance decide who should sleep with whom tonight?" "Very well," I said, "if it must be, we cannot refuse such an offer." It was decided to try it after the meal, and since we did not want to stay longer at table we stood up, and each walked up and down with his maiden. "No," said the Virgin, "this must not be: we will see how chance pairs us," whereupon we were separated again.

Now a dispute arose about how this should be done, but this was a premeditated plan, for the Virgin soon made the suggestion that we should mingle with one another in a ring; she would begin to count from herself, and every seventh one must take the next seventh for lover, be it man or maid. Since we saw no trick in it, we let it go ahead, thinking that we were well mixed up; but the maidens were so crafty that each one already knew her position. The Virgin began to count, and the seventh was another maiden; the next seventh, a maiden again, and so forth, to our astonishment, until every maiden was out, and none of us were hit upon! We poor souls were left standing all alone to suffer merciless teasing, and admit that we had been thoroughly foxed. If anyone had seen us in our ring, he would have thought it more likely for the heavens to fall than for the counting never to come to us. With this our games came to an end, and we had to be reconciled with the Virgin's practical joke.

Now wanton little Cupid came in again, but as a messenger from Their Majesties, who thereby sent us a drink in a golden beaker. He also summoned our maidens to attend the King, explaining that he could not tarry with them now, nor could we make sport with him. We let him fly off with the appropriate message of our humble thanks. Since in the meantime my companions' spirits had sunk to their feet, which the maidens were not sorry to see, they started up a gentle dance, which I preferred to watch rather than join. My mercurial friends, however, went to work on it as skilfully as if they had long learnt their trade. After a few dances, our President returned and told us that the artists and students had petitioned to honor and entertain Their Majesties before their departure by acting a pleasant comedy; and that if it was our desire to attend, we might accompany Their Majesties to the House of the Sun; that they would be pleased and would receive us graciously there. We first thanked them with the deepest humility for this honor, then prayed them to accept our unworthy service.

The Virgin took this message and returned with the command to await Their Majesties in our usual order in the gallery. We were led thither, and did not wait long, for the royal procession was already at hand, yet without any music. In front went the unknown Queen who had been with us yesterday, clothed in white satin with an elegant coronet; otherwise she carried nothing but a small crucifix made from a single pearl, which had been revealed today between the young King and his Bride. After her came the same six maidens as before, in two groups, carrying the King's regalia belonging to the little altar. Next came the three Kings with the Bridegroom in the middle, but he was quite plainly dressed, just in black satin, Italian style, and wearing a small round hat with a little black pointed feather. He doffed it to us courteously, to show his favor towards us, while we bowed (as we had to the previous one) as we had been instructed. After the Kings came the three Queens, of whom two were richly dressed. The one in the middle was also all in black, and Cupid carried her train. Here we were signalled to follow, and after us the maidens, until old Atlas brought up the rear.

In such procession we came at last through many an elegant walk to the House of the Sun, where we took our places near the King and Queen on a specially erected platform, to watch the comedy that had been prepared. We were on the right of the Kings, though separated from them, and the maidens on their left, except those in charge of the royal insignia, who were given a special place at the top. Any other servants had to stand below, between the pillars, and make the best of it.

Now since much in this comedy was strange and remarkable, I must not fail to give a brief summary of it.

[Act One] To begin with, an old King came out with several servants. A small chest was brought to his throne, with the news that it had been found on the water. When it was opened, there was a lovely baby, a few jewels, and a small letter on parchment, sealed and addressed to the King. He opened it immediately, but after he had read it broke into tears and informed his servants that the Moorish King had done him a great injury, seizing the lands of his kinswoman and murdering the entire royal lineage, right down to this infant. (He had previously intended to marry her daughter to his own son.) The King swore eternal enmity towards the Moor and his accomplices, and to wreak revenge. Then he ordered the baby to be nursed tenderly, and himself to be armed against the Moor. This preparation, and the girl's upbringing (for after she was a little older, she was put under an old tutor) lasted the whole first act, with many a fine and excellent diversion.

[First Interlude] Here a lion was set to fight a gryphon, and the lion won: which was very good to watch.

[Act Two] In the second act, the Moor came on, a spiteful black man. He had learnt to his fury that his massacre had been discovered, but that a little girl had been rescued from him by stealth. He wondered how he could counter so powerful an enemy by treachery, and was advised by some who had fled to him to escape famine. Against everyone's expectations, the girl fell into his clutches again, and he would certainly have had her strangled if he had not been cleverly deceived by his own servants. This act closed with a splendid triumph of the Moor.

[Act Three] In the third act, a great army was assembled by the King against the Moor, commanded by a brave old knight, who invaded the Moor's land and at last rescued the girl from the tower and clothed her again. After this they quickly raised a splendid platform and placed their young lady upon it. Soon came twelve royal messengers, among whom the same elderly knight made a speech, saying that his most gracious King had not only saved her from death before now, but had her raised in regal fashion, though she had not always behaved properly. Now he had chosen her before all others as wife to the young lord his son, and wished this wedding to take place without delay, so long as she would swear to him the following articles. Here he had read out from a parchment certain admirable conditions, which would be well worth recounting if it would not take too long. In brief, the maiden swore an oath to keep them faithfully, and thanked him most gracefully for this high favor. Then they all set to singing the praises of God, the King, and the maiden, and thus exited for the time being.

[Second Interlude] As a diversion, the four beasts of Daniel were brought on, as he saw them in his vision and minutely described them; all of which had a certain significance.

[Act Four] In the fourth act, the maiden was restored to her lost kingdom and crowned, and for a while was joyfully paraded in the courtyard with all ceremony. Many ambassadors presented themselves, not only to wish her well, but also to admire her finery. But her good conduct did not last for long: soon she was looking around herself saucily and winking at the ambassadors and other lords, in which she thoroughly acted out the role.

Her behavior soon came to the ears of the Moor, who did not want to let such an opportunity slip. Since her steward did not keep proper guard over her, she was easily seduced with extravagant promises, so that she lost her confidence in the King and secretly fell by degrees under the Moor's influence. Thereupon he made haste, and when he had brought her willingly into his power he charmed her with words until her whole kingdom became subject to him. Then, in the third scene of this act, he had her led out and stripped entirely naked, bound to a pillar on a rough wooden scaffold, well whipped, and finally condemned to death. This was so pitiful to see that many eyes ran over. Then she was thrust naked into the dungeon to await her death, which was to be by poison. It did not kill her, however, but left her completely leprous. So this act was largely tragic.

[Third Interlude] In between they brought out Nebuchadnezzar's image, decorated with many coats of arms on its head, breast, belly, thighs, feet, etc., which will also be discussed in the forthcoming interpretation.

[Act Five] In the fifth act the young King was told of all that had occurred between the Moor and his intended wife. First he made intercession for her with his father, pleading that she not be left in that condition. His father agreed to it, and legates were made ready to comfort her in her sickness and imprisonment, yet also to reprimand her for her indiscretion. But she would not receive them, consenting instead to be the Moor's concubine; which also occurred, and the young King was informed of it.

[Fourth Interlude] Now came a chorus of fools, each of them carrying a piece out of which they rapidly assembled a great globe of the world, and immediately demolished it again. This was a fine entertaining fantasy.

[Sixth Act] In the sixth act the young King decided to offer battle to the Moor, which took place, and the Moor was vanquished. Everyone thought that the young King was dead, too, but he recovered, freed his spouse, and prepared for his wedding, putting her under the guardianship of his steward and chaplain. The former greatly oppressed her until the tables were turned, and the padre became so bad and bold that he wanted all the power. When the young King was told of this, he instantly sent someone to break the padre's power, and to adorn bride, in moderation, for the wedding.

[Fifth Interlude] After the act a gigantic artificial elephant was brought out, which carried a great tower with musicians, to the delight of all.

[Act Seven] In the last act the Bridegroom appeared with almost incredible pomp, so that I wondered how such things were possible. The Bride came towards him with great solemnity, and all the people cried out *"Vivat Sponsus: Vivat Sponsa"* [Long live the Bridegroom! Long live the Bride!] Thus, through the comedy, they were all congratulating our King and Queen in the most courtly manner. All of which, as I later learned, pleased them extraordinarily.

Finally they all circled round once in a procession, till at last everyone began to sing as follows:

I.
This blessed time brings us such joy, with the King's wedding; therefore sing ye all and let it sound forth! Joy be his who bestows this on us.

II.
The lovely Bride whom we have awaited so long will now be betrothed to him. We have won what we have striven for. Happy is he who looks to himself.

III.
The goodly elders are now invited; long have they been cherished. Increase honorably, that thousands may arise from your own blood.

After this they took their leave, and so the comedy, especially pleasing to the Royal Persons, came to a happy end. Evening had almost come, so everyone departed in the same order; but we were to follow the Royal Persons up the spiral stair to the chamber I have spoken of. Here the tables were richly set, and it was the first time that we had been invited to the royal table. The little altar was placed in the middle of the room, and the six royal insignia were laid upon it. The young King conducted himself very graciously towards us, but he could not have been entirely happy because, though he sometimes talked a little with us, he frequently sighed. Little Cupid only scoffed and played his tricks.

The old King and Queen were very serious, and only the wife of one of the old ones showed any levity; I did not know why. The first table was occupied by the Royal Persons, and we sat by ourselves at the second. At the third were certain well-born maidens. All the other men and maidens had to wait. Everything was conducted with great state, but in such solemn stillness that I dare not say much about it. I must nonetheless mention that before the meal all the Royal Persons had put on shining snow-white clothing, and thus sat down at table. Above the table hung the same great golden crown, whose precious stones alone could well have sufficed to light the room. However, all the lights were kindled from the small taper on the altar: for what reason, I truly do not know. I certainly noticed that the young King several times sent food to the white snake on the altar, which also gave me something to think about. The chatter at this banquet was almost all young Cupid's, who could leave none of us alone, least of all myself, and was always coming up with some surprise. But there was no joy besides, and everything took place in silence. I could well imagine that some catastrophe was imminent. No music was to be heard; if any was asked a question, we replied in short, leaden words, and left it at that. In brief, everything had such a weird look about it that the sweat started to trickle down my body, and I think that the bravest man would have found his courage ebbing.

Now that this supper was almost at an end, the young King called for the book to be brought him from the altar, and opened it. Then he had an old man ask us once again whether we intended to stay by him for better or worse. We affirmed this, trembling, whereupon he asked us sorrowfully whether we would put our names to it. We had no choice but to consent, and so each had to stand up in turn and sign the book with his own hand. When this was done, the crystal fountain was brought forward, together with one very tiny glass, and all the Royal Persons drank from it, one after the other. Then it was handed to us, and so on to all the other people; and this was called the *Haustus Silentii* [Draught of Silence]. Hereupon all the Royal Persons gave us their hands, with the warning that if we did not henceforth stay by them, we would never see them again. At this our eyes truly ran over, but our President engaged herself solemnly on our behalf, which satisfied them.

Now a small bell was rung, at which the Royal Persons grew so pale that we almost despaired. Soon they were laying aside their white garments and dressing all in black; the whole hall was hung with black velvet, the floor covered with the same, and also the ceiling, this having all been prepared beforehand. Next the tables were removed and everyone sat round on the bench, ourselves also putting on black garments. Our President, who had been out, returned, bringing with her six satin bandages with which she bound the eyes of the six Royal Persons. Now that they could see nothing more, the servants speedily brought six covered coffins into the chamber and set them down, also placing a low black bench in the middle. Finally a tall man entered the room, black as coal, bearing in his hand a sharp ax.

First the old King was led to the bench, and his head was instantly struck off and wrapped in a black cloth. The blood, however, was caught in a great golden chalice and placed with him in the nearby coffin, which was covered and set aside. So it went with the others, till I thought it would be my turn next; but this did not occur, for as soon as the six Persons were beheaded, the black man began to leave. Another followed him, and just before the door he struck off the executioner's head, and brought it back together with the ax, both of which were laid in a small chest.

This seemed to me a very bloody wedding, but since I had no notion of what might happen next, I had to reserve judgment against the outcome. Our Virgin also told us to hold our peace, as some of us were getting faint-hearted and weeping. Then she said to us: "The life of these now rests in your hands; and if you follow me, you will see this death give life to many." With this she indicated that we should go to sleep, and give ourselves no further worry: they would surely receive their just reward. Thus she wished us all a good night, telling us that she herself must keep vigil with the corpses tonight. We consented, and each was led by his page to his own lodging. My page talked to me long and variously, which I remember well to this day, and again astonished me with his intelligence. When I finally realized that his intention was to lull me to sleep, I pretended to be sleeping soundly. But no sleep came to my eyes, and I could not forget the people who had been beheaded.

My lodging was situated facing the great lake, so that I could easily look out over it. The windows, too, were near the bed. At midnight, just as it had struck twelve, I suddenly noticed a great fire out on the lake. Frightened, I immediately opened the window to see what would transpire. Then I saw seven ships approaching from afar, all of them full of lights. Above each one floated a flame which moved hither and thither, sometimes sinking quite low, which I readily concluded must be the spirits of the beheaded. These ships gradually neared the shore, and each had but one man for crew. As soon as they came to land, I saw our Virgin going toward the ships with a torch, and after her the six covered coffins and the chest were each carried to a ship and stowed out of sight.

I woke my page, who thanked me much, since, having run about so much during the day, he would have slept right through this, though he knew all about it. As soon as the coffins were laid in the ships, all the lights were extinguished. The six flames traveled together over the lake, so that each ship had no more than a single warning light. There were also some hundreds of guards camped on the waterside, who despatched our Virgin back into the castle, where she carefully bolted everything up again. From this I guessed that nothing further would happen tonight, but that I must await the coming day, and so we went to bed again. I was the only one of my companions whose room had faced the lake, and who had seen this. Now I was tired out, and fell asleep in the midst of my manifold speculations.

The Fifth Day

The night was over, and the long awaited day had broken, when I hastily got out of bed, more because of my curiosity to know what would happen than because I had slept enough. After I had dressed I descended the stairs as usual, but it was still too early: I found no one else in the hall, so I asked my page to take me around the castle a little, and show me something unusual. As always, he did this willingly, and led me without delay down some steps beneath the ground to a great iron door, on which the following words were affixed in great copper letters.

bɼp ɛʐgɋ ∂pgʒx∂pö
ᴠɛɴᴠꜱ.
∂ɼp Ꞵɔhộö Ꞙꜱxɯʙόöxʊɔhpö
ʜộpööxö
vộögɛʊɔkphꜱ.ꞗpɋpö,vộö ɯòꞙxꜱɋ
gp∂ꜱxɔhɋ hxgɋ.

[*Hye lygt begraben / Venus, / dye schön Fraw, so manchen / Hoen man / umb glück, ehr, segen, und wolfart / gebracht hatt.* Here lies buried Venus, the fair woman who has undone many a great man in fortune, honor, blessing, and prosperity.]

I copied this and drew it on my writing-tablet. After the door was opened, the page led me by the hand through a very dark passage until we came to a small door which stood ajar. The page told me that it had first been opened yesterday when the coffins were taken out through it, and had not yet been locked. As we entered, I beheld the most precious thing ever created by Nature. This vault had no light but that of some enormous carbuncles; and it was, as I was informed, the King's Treasury. Of all the things I saw there, the most marvelous and extraordinary was a tomb that stood in the center, so rich that I wondered why it was not better guarded. The page answered that I should thank my planet, through whose influence I would now see some more things that no man had ever set eyes on, beside the King's household.

This tomb was triangular, having in the center a shiny copper vessel; the rest was of pure gold and precious stones. In the vessel stood an angel who held in his arms an unknown tree, from which fruits continually fell into the vessel. As soon as they dropped in, the fruits turned to liquid and flowed from there into three smaller golden vessels nearby. This little altar was supported by three beasts: Eagle, Ox, and Lion, all standing on a richly decorated base. I asked my page what this might mean: "Here lies buried Venus," he read, "the fair woman who has undone many a great man in fortune, honor, blessing, and prosperity." He showed me a copper door in the floor; "Here," he said, "we could descend further if you would like to." "I am still following you," said I, and with that I went down the stairs. It was very dark, but the page quickly opened a little box in which was an ever-burning light; from this he lit one of the many torches that lay to hand. I was very scared, and asked him earnestly if he should be doing this. He answered me: "Since the Royal Persons are still asleep, I have nothing to fear."

Now I saw a rich bed, ready made, hung about with fine curtains of which he opened one. And there I beheld the Lady Venus quite naked (for he also lifted the covers), lying there in such magnificence and beauty that I was paralyzed. To this day I do not know whether it was a statue or a dead person lying there, for she was completely still, and I dared not touch her. Then she was covered up again and the curtain was drawn. I still had her in my mind's eye, until I noticed a tablet behind the bed on which was written:

ωxö 6ːⲣ 'ʃsʋɔhɋ öⲣⳅ̈öℊƀ
dxʋös ωᴊsℊ ʋö88⪝öö̈ƀ,
ʋⲣsℬɔhö̈ⲣ8ⳅⲣö̈, ωⲣs6ⲣ ⳅɔh
xʋʃωxɔhⲣö ʋö6 ⲣⳅ̈ö
öʋℊⲣs 'ℬⲣⳅ̈ö ⲣⳅ̈öⲣƀ
ᴊ̇óöⳅℊℬ.

[Wan dye Frutcht meynes baums wyrt vollends verschmelzen, werde ych aufwachen und eyn muter seyn eynes konygs. When the fruit of my tree has completely melted, I shall awake and be the mother of a King.]

I asked my page about the inscription, but he laughed and promised that I would soon find out. Then he extinguished the torch and we climbed up again. Now that I could see all the little doors better, I found that at each corner a small pyrite taper was burning, which I had not noticed before, since the fire was so bright that it looked much more like a jewel than a light. The tree must have been continually melting from their heat, yet it kept bringing forth more fruits. "Now," said the page, "learn what I have heard Atlas reveal to the King: when the tree has completely melted, the Lady Venus will wake up again and be the mother of a King."

As he was speaking, and perhaps was going to tell me more, little Cupid flew in: he was at first rather upset at our presence, but when he saw that we looked more dead than alive, he had to laugh. He asked me what spirit had led me here, to which I answered trembling that I had got lost in the castle, and somehow ended up here; that the page had been looking for me everywhere, and had finally found me; and that I hoped he would not hold it against me. "No, it's all right," said Cupid, "my nosy old father! But you could easily have played me a nasty trick if you'd noticed this door. I must take better care of it." And with this he put a strong padlock on the copper door down through which we had climbed.

I thanked God that he had not discovered us earlier, and my page was even gladder that I had thus helped him out. "I still can't let it go," said Cupid, "that you nearly stumbled across my dear mother." With that he held the point of his arrow in one of the tapers until it was warm, then pricked me on the hand. I thought little of it at the time, but was happy that we had succeeded in coming through without further danger.

Meanwhile my companions had also got out of bed and were in the hall. I joined them there, making as though I had just got up. After Cupid had carefully locked everything up, he also joined us and made me show him my hand. There was still a little drop of blood there, which much amused him, and he advised the others that they should look out for me: I would soon be growing old! We all wondered how Cupid could be so cheerful and give no thought to the tragic events of yesterday. But he showed no sign of sorrow.

In the meantime, our President had made herself ready for the

journey. She entered all in black velvet, though still bearing her
laurel-branch, and all her maidens had laurel-branches, too. Since
everything was now ready, the Virgin told us first to take a drink,
then to get ready for the procession without delay. We were not long
about it, but followed her out of the hall into the courtyard. Here
the six coffins were standing, and my companions had no other
thought than that the six Royal Persons were lying within. I could
see right through the trick, but still did not know what would be
done with the others. By each coffin were eight masked men. As
soon as the music began (and it was such grave and tragic music that
I was awestruck), the men lifted up the coffins, and we followed
after, as instructed, as far as the garden mentioned above.

A wooden building was erected in the middle, with a splendid
crown around the roof, standing on seven columns. Inside were six
open graves, with a stone by each, and in the center a tall, round,
hollow stone. The coffins were laid in these graves, silently and
with much ceremony, and the stones were slid over them and
sealed fast. The little chest, however, was laid in the central one.
My companions were deceived by this, for they quite thought that
the corpses of the dead were inside. On top of all was a great banner
with the Phoenix painted on it, perhaps the better to delude us.
Here I had much to thank God for, that I had seen more than the
rest.

Now, after the burial was over, the Virgin stood up on the central
stone and made a short oration. She said that we should keep our
promise, and, not grudging future pains, should help the Royal
Persons thus entombed to come to life again. Therefore we were to
rise up forthwith and go with her to Olympus Tower, to fetch from
there the proper and indispensable medicines. We readily agreed,
and followed her through another little door as far as the waterfront.
There were the same seven ships, all empty, in which the maidens
planted their laurel-branches, and after they had distributed us in
the six ships, they sent us on our way in the name of God and
watched us until we were out of sight. Then they went back into
the castle with all the guards.

Each of our ships had a great banner and a special symbol. Five of
them had the five *Corpora Regularia* [regular or Platonic solids],

one apiece, while mine (in which the Virgin also sat) bore the
sphere. We sailed in a special order, and each had only two
crewsmen.

$$a \\ \| \\ b\| \ c\| \ d\| \\ e\|\ f\| \\ g\|$$

In front went the little ship (a) in which I suspected the Moor lay,
also containing twelve musicians who played very well; its symbol
was a pyramid. Then came three abreast (b, c, d), in which we were,
myself in (c). In the middle went the two finest and stateliest ships
(e, f); they had no one in them, but were trimmed with many laurel-
branches, and their banners were the sun and moon. Last (g) came
a single ship in which were forty maidens.

After passing over the lake, we came through a narrow channel
to the sea itself, where all the sirens, nymphs, and sea-goddesses
were awaiting us. A mermaid immediately came to us from them
to bring us their gift, and in honor of the wedding: it was a huge,
precious, set pearl, whose like has never been seen either in ours or
in the New World, round and lustrous. After the Virgin had
graciously accepted it, the nymph asked her if we would anchor for
a while and be an audience to their games; to which the Virgin also
agreed. She had the two large ships heave to in the center, and the
others make a pentagon around them.

$$c \\ b\nearrow \ = \ \searrow d \\ e\| \ \|f \\ g\nwarrow \ /\!/a$$

Then the nymphs swam round in a circle, singing with their
lovely voices the following song:

I

On earth there's nothing better
Than fair and noble Love,
Through which we are made godlike,

And none does other harm.
Therefore sing unto the King,
Make the whole sea to resound,
We ask you—answer us.

II

Who has brought us to life?
  'Tis Love.
Who has restored us grace?
  'Tis Love.
From whence have we our birth?
  From Love.
What could lead us astray?
  No Love.

III

Who has begotten us?
  'Twas Love.
Why did they give us suck?
  From Love.
What is our parents' due?
  Our Love.
Why are they patient so?
  From Love.

IV

What overcometh all?
  'Tis Love.
Can one find love as well?
  Through Love.
How can one do good work?
  In Love.
Who can unite the twain?
  'Tis Love.

V

So sing ye all,
Echoing loud,
In honor of Love,
Which will increase
Unto our lords the King and Queen;

Their bodies are here; their souls are gone.

VI

And while we live,
So God will grant
That as from us homage and love
Have sundered them with mighty power,
So may we too, through flame of love
With joy unite them once again.

VII

This sorrow, then,
To greatest joy,
Though many thousand generations come,
Shall be transformed for all eternity.

After they had finished this song with its beautiful words and melody, I no more wondered at Ulysses for having stopped his companions' ears, for I thought myself the most unhappy of men that nature had not made me an equally blissful creature. But the Virgin soon took her leave of them, and bade us sail away from there. Hence also the nymphs, after they had been presented with a long red ribbon in recompense, broke ranks and scattered in the sea.

At this time I became aware that Cupid was also beginning to work on me, which was really not to my credit; but since to tell of my deception would be of no use to the reader, I will let it go at that. It was the very head-wound which I had received in my dream in the First Book. If any would be warned by me, let him not loiter around Venus' bed, for Cupid cannot abide that kind of thing.

After a few hours, when we had sailed a good way in friendly conversation, we espied Olympus Tower. Then the Virgin ordered some cannons to be fired as a sign of our arrival. Immediately we saw a great white flag run up, and a little golden boat coming towards us. When it arrived, there was an old gentleman, the Warder of the Tower, with some halberdiers dressed in white, by whom we were welcomed as friends and thus led to the Tower. This stood on a perfectly square island, surrounded by such a strong and thick rampart that I myself counted two hundred and sixty steps as we passed through it. Beyond the rampart was a fine meadow with some gardens, in which grew strange fruits unknown to me; then a wall around the Tower. The Tower itself was just as if seven round towers had been built together, but the central one was a little taller. They were all connected inside, and had seven stories.

As we came up to the gate of the Tower, they led us by the wall, a little off to the side. I could well see that it was so as to bring the coffins into the Tower without our knowledge, but the others knew nothing of this. As soon as it was done, they took us into the lowest part of the Tower. Although it was finely painted, we did not have much diversion here, since this was nothing else than a laboratory. We had to grind and wash herbs, gemstones, and whatnot, extracting the sap and essence, then put it in little bottles and hand them over to be preserved. Our Virgin was so industrious and organizing, she knew how to keep each one fully employed. We had to drudge away on this island until we had done everything necessary for reviving the beheaded bodies. In the meantime (as I later learned), the three maidens were in the first room, and were diligently washing the corpses. Finally, as we were almost finished with these preparations, they gave us nothing but some broth and a drink of wine—from which I could clearly see that we were not here for our amusement. Moreover, when we had finished our day's work, each one had only a blanket spread on the floor, and we had to make the best of it.

I was not much tempted to sleep, and so went out for a walk in the garden, coming eventually to the rampart. Since the skies were so clear, I could happily pass the time in contemplation of the stars. I accidentally came upon a great stone staircase which led onto the rampart, and since the moon was shining very brightly, I was bold enought to go up and look a while over the sea, which was now utterly calm. Having such a good opportunity for astronomical contemplations, I discovered that on this very night there was a conjunction of planets such as would not be seen again for a long time.

After I had looked out to sea a good while, and it being around midnight, as soon as it had struck twelve I saw the seven flames coming from the distance over the sea until they reached the very top of the Tower. This somewhat frightened me, for as soon as the flames had come to land, the wind began to make the sea very rough. The moon was hidden by clouds, and my pleasure ended in such fear that I scarcely had time to find the staircase again and get back into the Tower. Whether the flames now stayed there, or whether they went away again, I cannot say, for I would never have dared venture out in such darkness. So I lay on my blanket and fell asleep all the sooner, since in our laboratory there was a fountain with a gentle murmuring sound. Thus the fifth day also ended with wonders.

The Sixth Day

Next morning, after we had woken one another, we sat together a while to talk about what would come of all this. Some thought that they would all return to life together. Others, on the contrary, thought that the death of the old ones would afford the young ones not only life, but increase. Others again believed that they had not been killed, but that different people had been beheaded in their place.

After we had discussed it together for some time, the old gentleman entered, greeted us, and looked around to see if all was ready and the procedures carried out sufficiently. Our conduct had been such that he could find no fault with our diligence, and so he collected all the glasses together and packed them in a case. Soon a few youths came in, bringing with them several ladders, ropes, and large wings which they laid down in front of us, and went out again. The old gentleman then began: "Dear sons, each must carry one of these three objects all day; but you are free either to choose one for yourselves, or to draw lots for them."

We said that we would like to choose. "No," replied the old gentleman, "it must be done by lot." Thereupon he made three tickets, on which he wrote respectively "Ladder," "Rope," and "Wings." These he placed in a hat, and each had to draw one, and that would be his. Those who got the ropes thought that they were best off, but I had a ladder, which annoyed me very much as it was twelve feet long and quite heavy. I had to carry it, whereas the others could wind their flexible ropes around themselves. For the third group, the old gentleman fixed on their wings as neatly as if they had grown there.

Now he turned off a tap, and the fountain stopped running; we then had to remove it from the middle of the room. After everything had been cleared away, he took the case with the glasses and left, locking the door fast after him, so that we could only think that we were imprisoned in this tower. But before a quarter of an hour had passed, a round hole was opened high up, and there we saw our Virgin, who called to us, wished us good day, and invited us to come up. The ones with wings were quickly through the opening, and we others soon saw what our ladders were for; only the ones with ropes were in trouble, for as soon as one of us arrived up there, he was told to draw his ladder up after him. At last each hung his rope on an iron hook, then had to climb up it, which was not to be done without blisters.

When we were all up, the opening was closed again and the Virgin gave us a kindly greeting. This room was as big as the tower and had six attractive chambers a little higher than the room, into which one had to climb by three steps. We were distributed in these chambers to pray for the lives of the King and Queen. Meanwhile the Virgin went in and out of the little door until we were ready.

As soon as we had finished our business, a peculiar, longish object was brought through the little door and placed in the middle by twelve persons (who had formerly been our musicians). My companions took it for a still, but I could well see that the corpses lay inside it, for the chest beneath it was rectangular, and easily big enough for six persons to lie inside. Then they went out again, fetched their instruments, and accompanied our Virgin and her maidservants with beautiful music.

The Virgin carried a little chest, the rest only branches and small lamps, and some of them lighted torches. Then we were also given torches to hold, and were made to stand around the fountain.

First stood the Virgin (A) with her maids around her in a circle, with their lamps and branches (c). Then we stood with the torches (b); next the musicians were in a row (a), and the other maidens also in a row (d). I did not know where these maidens had come from: whether they lived in the Tower, or whether they had been brought there in the night, for all their faces were hidden with fine white veils, so that I could not recognize any of them.

Now the Virgin opened the little chest, in which was a round object wrapped in thick green satin. She laid this in the upper vessel, and covered it with a lid that was full of holes, and had a rim on which she poured some of the fluids that we had prepared yesterday. The still immediately began to flow, the liquid running back into the little vessel through four tubes. Under the lower vessel were many spikes on which the maidens hung their lamps, so that the heat came into the vessel and made the water simmer. When the water boiled, there were many small holes through which it could fall in on the corpses, and it was so hot that it dissolved all the bodies and turned them to liquid. My companions did not yet know what the round, wrapped-up thing above was, but I understood that it was the Moor's head, from which the water took on such extreme heat. Around the large vessel there were many holes in which the branches were stuck, though I did not know whether this was necessary, or just a ritual. However, these branches were continually sprinkled by the still, and the drips that returned from them into the vessel were somewhat more yellow.

The still had been running of its own accord for nearly two hours, but more feebly the longer it went. In the meantime the musicians broke ranks, and we walked about in the room, which was so set up that we had ample means of passing the time. Nothing had been omitted in the way of images, paintings, clocks, organs, running fountains, and the like. At last it came to the point at which the still would run no longer, whereupon the Virgin had a round golden sphere brought in. At the bottom of the still was a tap, through which she let all the matter that had been dissolved by those hot drops run into the sphere, a portion of which was very red. The other water remained above in the vessel, and was poured out. Then this still, which had now become much lighter, was taken out again. I myself cannot say whether it was opened outside, or whether anything further of value remained of the corpses; but I do know that the water that was collected in the sphere was much heavier, for it took six or more of us to carry it, though by its size it should not have been too heavy for one.

After this sphere had with difficulty been taken out through the door, we were left sitting alone again, but when I heard a coming and going above us, I had an eye to my ladder. One would have heard my companions give strange opinions about this still, for since they could not imagine the corpses to be anywhere but in the castle garden, they could not evaluate this process. But I thanked God that I had woken at such an opportune time, and seen that which helped me better in everything the Virgin did.

After a quarter of an hour the cover above us was opened, and we were commanded to come up, which we did as before with wings, ladders, and ropes. It annoyed me somewhat that the maidens must have gone up by another way, while we had to work so hard; but I realized that there was something special about it, and also that we had to leave the old gentleman something to do. Even those with wings had no advantage, except when they came to pass through the opening. When we had got up there, and the aperture had been closed, I saw the sphere in the middle of the room, hanging by a strong chain. There was nothing in this room but plain windows, and between each pair of them a door, which concealed nothing but a great polished mirror. These windows and mirrors were placed opposite each other for optical effect, such that when the sun (now shining more brightly than usual) met just one of the doors, nothing but sun was visible throughout the whole room, so long as the window facing the sun was open, and the doors in front of the mirrors likewise. Through artificial reflection they all shone onto the golden sphere which hung in the center, and since this too was highly polished, it gave off such a blaze that none of us could keep his eyes open. We had to look out of the windows until the sphere was well heated and the desired effect achieved. Here I must say that in this mirroring I beheld the most wonderful thing that Nature ever brought to light: for everywhere there were suns, but the sphere in the center shone even brighter, so that like the sun we could not bear to look at it for a moment.

At last the Virgin commanded the mirrors to be closed again and the windows shut, so that the sphere could cool off a little; and this occurred towards seven o'clock. We thought this was good, since we could now have a vacation and refresh ourselves a little with breakfast. But this collation was extremely philosophical, and we had no need to worry about intemperance—yet we were not starved. The hope of coming joy, with which the Virgin continually comforted us, made us so happy that we gave no heed to labor or inconvenience. I can also say this truly of my illustrious companions: that they never thought of kitchen or table, but their pleasure was only in the pursuit of such adventurous physics, and in the contemplation therein of the Creator's wisdom and omnipotence.

After we had taken our meal, we settled down to work again, for the sphere had sufficiently cooled. With great trouble and difficulty we had to lift it off the chain and onto the floor. Now came the debate over how we were to divide it, because our instructions were to cut it apart in the middle. A sharp diamond turned out to be best in the end. When we opened the sphere, there was nothing red inside it, but a beautiful, large, snow-white egg. It pleased us immensely that it had turned out so well, for the Virgin was always worrying that the shell might still be too fragile. We stood around this egg with as much joy as if we had laid it ourselves! But the Virgin soon had it removed, disappeared herself, and as always locked the door. I do not know whether she did something out there with the egg, or whether something clandestine was done to it, but I do not believe so. We, however, had to wait by ourselves for a quarter of an hour until the third hole was opened, and we came by means of our apparatus to the fourth storey or floor.

In this chamber we found a great copper vessel filled with yellow sand, warmed by a gentle fire, in which the egg was buried so as to come to full maturity. This vessel was square, and on one side these two verses were written in large letters:

O.BLI.TO.BIT.MI.LI.
KANT.I.VOLT.BIT.TO.GOLT.

On the other side were these three words:

SANITAS.NIX.HASTA.
[Health; Snow; Lance]

The third had nothing but the single word:

F.I.A.T.
[So be it]

But on the back was a whole inscription, reading as follows:

QUOD.
Ignis: Aër: Aqua: Terra:
SANCTIS REGUM ET REGINARUM NOSTR:
Cineribus.
Eripere non potuerunt.
Fidelis Chymicorum Turba.
IN HANC URNAM
Contulit.
Ad.

[What Fire, Air, Water, Earth, could not rob from the holy ashes of our Kings and Queens, the faithful flock of alchemists has gathered in this urn. AD 1459.]

I leave it for the learned to argue about whether the sand or the egg was meant by this. I will do my part, and leave nothing unsaid. Now our egg was ready, and was taken out. It needed no cracking, for the bird inside soon extracted itself, and appeared quite happy although it looked very bloody and unformed. We placed it first on the warm sand, and the Virgin said that before anything was given it to eat, we should tie it up, otherwise it would give us all trouble aplenty. This was done, then food was brought to it, which was surely none other than the blood of the beheaded people, diluted again with prepared water. The bird grew so fast beneath our very eyes that we could understand why the Virgin had warned us about it: it bit and scratched about itself so fiercely that if anyone had fallen into its clutches it would soon have done away with him. Now it was quite black and wild, and so another food was brought for it—perhaps the blood of another Royal Person—whereupon all the black feathers fell out again, and in their place there grew snow-white plumage. Then it became somewhat tamer and easier to deal with, though we still did not trust it. With the third meal, its feathers began to become colored, and so beautiful that in all my life I have never seen colors to compare. By now the bird was extremely docile and so friendly towards us that with the Virgin's consent we let it out of captivity.

"Now," she began, "since through your hard work and our old gentleman's permission the bird has been endowed with life and great perfection, it is proper for us to give it a joyful consecration." Thereupon she ordered lunch to be brought in, and us to relax, since now the most demanding work was over and it was fitting for us to enjoy our past labors. We began to be merry together, though we still had on our mourning clothes, which seemed to make rather a mockery of our joy. The Virgin kept asking questions, perhaps to find out which of us would be best served by her forthcoming scheme. She was mostly concerned with smelting, and was very pleased when she found someone adept at the fine manipulations which distinguish an artist. This luncheon lasted no longer than three-quarters of an hour, most of which we spent with our bird, which we constantly had to feed with its food; but now it stayed the same size.

We were not left very long to digest our meal, but after the Virgin had gone away, together with the bird, the fifth chamber was opened to us, where we offered our services after getting there in the accustomed way. In this room, a bath was prepared for our bird, colored with a fine white powder so as to look like pure milk. It was cool at first, and when the bird was put in it enjoyed it, drinking out of it and playing around. But then it began to be heated by the lamps placed underneath, and we had trouble keeping the bird in the bath. So we clapped a lid on the vessel, but let it stick its head out through a hole. In this bath it shed all its feathers and became as smooth as a human being; also the heat no longer hurt it. This amazed me, since all its feathers were consumed in this bath, coloring the water blue. At length we gave the bird air, and it sprang out of the vessel by itself, so shining smooth that it was a delight to see. But since it was still somewhat wild, we had to put a collar with a chain round its neck, and thus led it up and down the room. Meanwhile, a strong fire was lit under the vessel, and the bath was boiled away until it turned all to a blue stone, which we took out and crushed; then we had to grind it on a stone, and finally paint the bird's skin all over with the resulting color. Now it looked stranger still, for it was blue all over except for its head, which stayed white.

Now all our work on this floor was completed, so after the Virgin had left with our blue bird, we were summoned through the opening to the sixth floor, whither we went. Here we were much troubled, for in the middle there stood an altar, exactly as described above in the King's hall; on it stood the six objects I have mentioned, and the bird itself made a seventh. First the little fountain was set before it, from which it drank a good draught. Then it pecked the white snake until it was badly bleeding. We had to collect this blood in a golden beaker, and pour it down the throat of the bird, who resisted violently. Next we dipped the snake's head into the fountain, so that it came back to life and crept into its death's-head, after which I saw nothing of it for a long time. Meanwhile the sphere was moving ever forward until it made the desired conjunction, and the little clock immediately struck one. Thereupon followed another conjunction, and the clock struck two. Finally, as we observed the third conjunction and it was signaled by the clock, the poor bird submissively laid its neck on the book, and willingly allowed its head to be struck off by one of us, chosen for this by lot. It gave forth not a drop of blood until its breast was opened, when the blood spurted out as fresh and clear as if it had been a fountain of rubies.

Its death touched us to the heart, yet we could not imagine that a mere bird would help us much, so we let it be. We cleared it off the altar and helped the Virgin burn it to ashes, together with the small tablet hanging nearby, with fire lit from the taper. The ashes were purified several times and carefully preserved in a box of cypress wood.

Here I cannot conceal what a trick was played on me and three others. After we had carefully put away the ashes, the Virgin began thus:

"Dear sirs, We are now in the sixth chamber, and have only one more before us, in which our labors will be at an end; we will travel back to our castle, to awaken our most gracious Lords and Ladies. I would have wished that all of you, gathered together here, had conducted yourselves in such a way that I could have commended you to our most worthy King and Queen, and that you might have received a fitting reward. But these four (here she pointed to me and three others) have proved, against my wishes, to be lazy and indolent workers.

"However, because of my charity towards one and all, I do not want to deliver them to their well-deserved punishment; yet so that such idleness shall not remain wholly unpunished, I propose this for them: they alone shall be excluded from the forthcoming seventh operation, the most wondrous of all; but they will not need to make further atonement afterwards, before Their Majesties."

I leave others to imagine how I felt after this speech, for the Virgin was able to look so serious that the floods overflowed and we thought ourselves the most miserable of all men. Then the Virgin had the musicians called by one of the maidservants (of whom there were always many at hand), and they with their cornets had to play us out of the door, with such mockery and derision that they could scarcely blow for laughing. What hurt us especially was that the Virgin herself found our tears, anger, and impatience so amusing, and that among our companions there may have been some who enjoyed our discomfiture.

But it turned out quite differently. For as soon as we were out of the door, the musicians told us to cheer up and follow them up the spiral stair that led past the seventh storey to beneath the roof. There we found the old gentleman, whom we had not seen hitherto, standing on a little round furnace. He received us kindly and congratulated us heartily on being thus chosen by the Virgin. But when he understood the fright we had received, he almost burst himself laughing at us for having taken our good fortune so ill. "So, dear sons, learn from this," he said, "that man never knows what good things God intends for him."

As he was speaking, the Virgin came running in with her box, and after she was done laughing at us, she emptied the ashes into another container, and filled hers up again with a different substance, explaining that she must now throw some sand in the other artists' eyes; but that we should do as the old gentleman told us, and especially not let our efforts flag. Thereupon she left us for the seventh room, into which she summoned our companions. What she first did with them there, I cannot tell, for not only were they strictly forbidden to say, but because of our duties we did not dare to spy on them through the ceiling. Our work was as follows: we had to saturate the ashes with our previously prepared water until they became a thin paste. Then we set the material on the fire until it was well heated. While it was hot, we poured it out into two little forms or molds, and let it cool slightly.

Now we had a moment to spy on our companions through some cracks. They were busy with an oven, each one having to blow the fire himself with a pipe. Around they stood, blowing fit to burst, but still thinking it wonderful how much better off they were than us. This blowing went on so long that our old gentleman called us back to work, so I do not know what happened afterwards.

We opened up the molds, and there were two beautiful, bright, and almost transparent images such as human eyes have never seen, of a little boy and girl, each only four inches long. What amazed me the most was that they were not hard, but as soft and fleshlike as any human being; but they had no life. I am quite certain that the Lady Venus' image was made in some such way. These babies, lovely as angels, we laid first on two satin cushions, and gazed at them for a long time, reduced to idiocy by such an enchanting spectacle. But the old gentleman roused us and told us continually to let one drop after another of the bird's blood, which had been caught in the golden beaker, fall into the images' mouths. This apparently made them grow, and whereas they had started out tiny, now they grew more beautiful in proportion to their size. Would that all painters could have been here, to be ashamed of their art in the face of these creations of Nature!

Now they were getting so big that we lifted them off the cushions and had to lay them on a long table covered with white velvet, as the old gentleman directed us, and covered them as far as the chest with a soft white satin sheet. They were so inexpressibly beautiful that we did this almost reluctantly. In short, before we had used up all the blood, they were already fully grown, and both had curly golden-yellow hair. The image of Venus was nothing to them. But there was no natural warmth there, no feeling: they were dead images, yet lively and natural in color. For fear that they might grow too big, the old gentleman had them fed no more, but pulled the sheet up over their faces and had the table stuck around with torches.

Here I must warn the reader not to think of these lights as necessary, for the old gentleman's intention was merely that we should not see when the souls went into them. We would not have noticed it, if I had not twice before seen the flames; but I let the other three rest in their belief, nor did the old gentleman know that I had seen anything more.

Hereupon he asked us to sit down on a bench opposite the table, and presently the Virgin came in with the musicians and all the apparatus. She carried two beautiful white garments of a sort I had never seen in the castle, nor can I describe them, for I could only think that they were of pure crystal, only soft and opaque. That is all I can say about them. She laid them down on a table, and after setting her maidens around on the bench, she and the old gentleman began to do a lot of conjuring round the table, which was only to confuse us. This happened, as I have said, under the roof, which was made in a remarkable way: inside there were seven concave hemispheres; the middle one was somewhat higher and had at the top a small round hole which was closed, and which none of the others had observed.

After much ceremony six maidens came in, each carrying a large trumpet that was wound round with a green, fiery, luminous material, like a wreath. The old gentleman took one of them, and after removing some of the lights at the head of the table and uncovering the faces, he set a trumpet in one of the mouths so that the upper and wider part came exactly to the roof-vent. My companions were staring only at the bodies, but I had other thoughts, for as soon as the foliage or wreath around the tube was kindled, I saw the hole above open and a bright stream of fire shoot through the tube and pass into the body. Then the hole was shut again and the trumpet removed, through which trick my companions were deceived into thinking that life had entered the image through the fire of the foliage. As soon as the soul was received, the body opened and closed its eyes, but scarcely moved. Again he placed another tube on its mouth, lit it, and the soul was let down through the tube; and this happened three times to each. Then all the lights were extinguished and removed, the velvet tablecloth folded over the bodies, and a double-bed set up and prepared, on which the wrapped bodies were placed. They were taken out of the coverings, laid neatly side by side, and left to sleep a good while with the curtains drawn.

Now it was time for the Virgin to see how our other artists were faring. They were quite happy, for, as the Virgin later told me, they were having to work in gold (which is also a part of this art, though not the noblest, the most necessary, or the best). They also had a portion of these ashes, and were firmly convinced that the whole bird was provided for the sake of gold, and that thus the dead bodies would be brought back to life. Meanwhile we sat silently waiting for our couple to awaken, which took place after about half an hour. Now cheeky Cupid came in again and, after greeting each of us, flew in under the bed-curtain and pestered them until they awoke. This caused them great astonishment, for they thought that they had simply slept from the moment they were beheaded until now. Cupid, after he had woken them and introduced them to one another again, stepped aside a little and let the two of them recover somewhat. Then he aimed his tricks at us, and in the end we were obliged to fetch the musicians for him and to be more cheerful. Not long afterwards the Virgin herself entered, and after she had humbly greeted the young King and Queen (who still felt rather weak), and kissed their hands, she brought them the two beautiful garments I mentioned, which they put on and thus stepped forward. Now two fine seats had been made ready, and there they sat, to be greeted by us with the deepest submission. The King, in his own person, most graciously thanked us and again assured us of his favor.

It was already about five o'clock, and they could not stay longer, but as soon as the most important things could be loaded, we led the young Royal Persons down the spiral staircase, through all the doors and guards, to the ship. There they embarked together with some of the maidens and Cupid, and sailed away so swiftly that we soon lost sight of them. But I was told that they were met by many stately ships, and that in four hours they had traversed many miles of sea.

After five o'clock, the musicians were told to take everything back onto the ships, and to prepare for departure. But since it was going rather slowly, the old gentleman for the first time brought out some of his secret soldiers, who up to now had been hidden in the ramparts so that we had seen none of them. From this I could tell that the Tower was well provided against opposition. These soldiers made short work of our stuff, so there was soon no more to be done than to eat supper.

The table was already set, as the Virgin brought us back to our companions. We had to look downcast and keep from laughing, but they smiled at one another, though a few of them were sorry for us. The old gentleman was also with us at supper, and a keen inspector he was: none could say anything so clever that he would not either turn it around, or cap it, or at least give some good information about it. I learnt a great deal from this gentleman, and it would be excellent if everyone were to go to him and learn his business, then things would often not turn out so badly.

After we had eaten supper, the old gentleman led us first into his cabinets of curiosities here and there in the bastions. There we saw such marvels of Nature, and other things imitated from Nature by the human mind, that even a year would not have sufficed us. We examined them by lamplight far into the night. At last, when we desired sleep more than seeing any further strange thing, we were led to our quarters and there, in the rampart, had not only fine, comfortable beds but unusually elegant rooms. This made us wonder all the more why we had been made to suffer so yesterday. I slept well in my bedroom, and since I was largely unworried, and weary from constant working, the soft rushing of the sea helped me to a sound and gentle sleep, and I continued in a dream from eleven o'clock at night until eight in the morning.

The Seventh Day

After eight o'clock I woke and quickly got myself ready, intending to go back to the Tower. But the dark passages in the rampart were so many and various that I wandered a good while before finding an exit. This happened to others, too, until at last we met in the lowest vault and were given clothes all of yellow, as well as our Golden Fleeces. At this time the Virgin told us that we were Knights of the Golden Stone, which we had not known beforehand. When we were all ready and breakfasted, the old gentleman presented each one with a golden medal, on one side of which were these words:

AR.NAT.MI.
[*Ars naturae ministra*: Art is the minister of Nature]

On the other side were these:

TEM.NA.F.
[*Temporis natura filia*: Nature is the daughter of Time]

He exhorted us to take nothing over and beyond these mementos. Then we went out to the sea again, where our ships lay, so splendidly appointed that it was scarcely possible: such beautiful things must have been brought there beforehand. There were twelve ships: six of ours and six of the old gentleman's, the latter all manned with smartly turned-out soldiers. He himself came on our ship, where we were all together. In the first sat the musicians, of which the old gentleman had a great number, sailing in front of us to make the time pass more pleasantly. Our flags were the twelve signs of the zodiac, and we were in Libra. Among other things, our ship had a very lovely clock which showed all the minutes; and the sea was so calm that it was a great pleasure to sail on it. Best of all was the old gentleman's discourse. He told us wonderful stories to pass the time, so that I could happily have traveled with him my life long. Meanwhile, the ships went quite speedily, and before two hours had passed, the sailor told us that he could already see almost the whole lake covered with ships. As soon as we left the sea and came through the channel into the lake, there were about five hundred vessels, among them one sparkling with pure gold and gemstones in which sat the King and Queen with many noble lords, ladies, and maidens.

As soon as they saw us, all the cannons on both sides were fired, and there was such a din of trombones, trumpets, and kettledrums that all the ships on the lake shuddered. Finally, as we arrived they surrounded our ships and we hove to. Straightway, old Atlas came aboard on the King's behalf, made a short but eloquent speech in which he bade us welcome, and asked whether the royal gift was ready. My other companions wondered greatly how this King had resurrected, for they thought that they would have to reawaken him. But we left them in their confusion and made as if we did not understand, either. After Atlas' speech, our old gentleman came forward and responded with a somewhat longer oration, in which he wished the King and Queen all joy and increase, then handed over a small decorated casket. But what was in it, I did not know. Cupid alone was entrusted with it, as he flitted around between the two of them. When the speech was over, a salvo was fired, and we sailed together for a while until at last we came to another waterfront.

This was near the first gate, by which I had originally entered. On the square a great crowd of the royal household was waiting, together with several hundred horse. As soon as we docked and landed, the King and Queen offered each of us their hand with especial courtesy, and we were all mounted on horseback. Here I would ask my friendly reader not to take this narrative as pride or self-glorification, but to believe that if it were not strictly necessary, I would much prefer to have kept silent about the honor shown to me. We were all distributed among the Lords, but our old gentleman and my unworthy self had to ride beside the King, each of us carrying a snow-white standard with a red cross. My treatment was surely due to my age, for both of us had long grey beards and hair. I had fastened my tokens around my hat, which the young King soon noticed, asking whether I was the one who was able to redeem the tokens beneath the portal. I answered humbly "Yes"; but he laughed at me, and told me I should need no decoration from now on: I was his father! Then he asked me what I had redeemed them with. I answered: "with Water and Salt," whereupon he asked who had made me so wise. Then I grew bolder and told him what had happened with my bread, the dove, and the raven. He was pleased, but said expressly that God must have given me extraordinarily good fortune in this.

Now we came to the first portal, where the blue-clad porter stood holding a petition in his hand. As soon as he saw me beside the King he handed me the petition, humbly entreating that I would remind the King of the porter's kindness to me. First I asked the King how it stood with this porter. He answered me in a friendly way that he used to be a famous and skilled astrologer, held in great honor by the King's father, but that he had once offended the Lady Venus, and seen her in her bed. As punishment for this he was made to guard the first portal until someone should release him from it. I asked whether he could now be released. The King said: "Yes, if someone can be found who has committed as great a sin as he; they can take his place, and he will be free."

These words cut me to the quick, for my conscience convinced me that I was the offender. But I kept silent and handed over the petition. As soon as the King had read it, he was so alarmed that the Queen, who was riding behind us with her maidens and another Queen (whom I remembered from the hanging of the weights), noticed it and asked him what this letter meant. But he had not wanted anything to be noticed, and, putting away the letter, began to talk of other things until we came to the castle at about three o'clock.

When we had dismounted and accompanied the King into his hall, he called old Atlas to join him in a small closet and showed him the letter. Atlas lost no time in riding away, back to the porter, to find out more about this matter. The young King sat down with his wife and other lords, ladies, and maidens. Then our Virgin began to praise loudly our diligence, trouble, and labors, with the request that we be royally rewarded, and that she might enjoy the benefit of her commission from then on. The old gentleman also stood up and, confirming all that the Virgin had spoken, said that it would be only just for us all to receive satisfaction. Now we were told to step out for a while, and each to make a feasible wish, which would be granted; for there was no doubt that the wisest would make the best wish. We were to think about it until after dinner.

Now the King and Queen began to play a game with each other, to pass the time. It resembled chess, but had different rules: it was between the Virtues and the Vices, and it was pretty to see what traps the Vices set for the Virtues, and how they could be countered. The game was so clever and ingenious that I wished we had it, too. During the game, Atlas returned and delivered his message secretly. I went red from head to foot, for my conscience left me no peace. The King told me to read the petition for myself, whose contents were roughly as follows: first, the porter wished the King prosperity and increase, that his seed should be spread far and wide. Then he indicated that the day had now come when, according to the royal promise, he should be relieved. If his observations did not deceive him, Venus had already been discovered by one of his guests. If His Majesty would make keen and diligent inquiry, he would find that his discovery was true; and if none such were to be found, he would remain by the gate for the rest of his life. He then requested most humbly that if, in peril of his life and limb, he were permitted to attend dinner tonight, he would hope to identify the miscreant himself and thus earn the freedom he desired. All this was explicitly and eloquently put, so that I could well appreciate the porter's ingenuity; but it was too painful for me, and I would prefer never to have set eyes on it. I wondered whether I could help myself out of it through my wish, so I asked the King whether the porter could be released in any other way. "No," answered the King, "for there is a special consideration in this matter; but we may well concede his request for this evening. Send someone out to fetch him here." Meanwhile, tables were being set in a room where we had never been before: it was so perfect and well furnished that I cannot begin to describe it. We were conducted in with particular pomp and ceremony. Cupid was not here this time, for, as I learned, he was rather angry at the affront his mother had received. In short, my action and the porter's petition were a matter for great sorrow. The King hesitated to institute an enquiry among all his guests, for then those who knew nothing of the matter would find out about it. So as soon as the porter arrived, he let the man himself look sharply around him, while the King behaved as cheerfully as he could.

At last people began to be merrier, and to make all kinds of interesting and diverting conversation. There is no need to tell the reader all about the feast and other ceremonies, for that is not what I intend; but everything was beyond measure, thanks more to art and human skill than to the fact that we had drunk heavily. This was the last and most splendid meal we had attended. After the banquet, the tables were quickly cleared and some elegant chairs put round in a circle in which we were to sit, together with the King and Queen, the two old men, the ladies and maidens. A handsome page now opened the wonderful little book mentioned earlier. Atlas placed himself in the midst and began to read from it to us, to the effect that His Majesty had not forgotten what we had done for him, and how diligently we had discharged our duties; therefore, as a reward, he appointed each and every one of us a Knight of the Golden Stone. We were to note that henceforth we must not only submit to His Majesty, but hold to the following articles; thus His Majesty would also know how to behave towards his liegemen. Then Atlas had the page read the articles, which were these:

1. You Lord Knights shall swear to ascribe your Order not to any devil or spirit, but only to God your Creator, and to Nature, his handmaiden.

2. You shall abominate all whoredom, incontinence, and uncleanness, and not defile your Order with such vices.

3. Through your gifts you shall willingly come to the aid of all who are deserving and in need.

4. You shall not desire this honor to use it for worldy show or high esteem.

5. You shall not wish to live longer than God wills.

We had to laugh at this last article, which was perhaps put in only as a joke. We now had to swear to them all on the King's scepter, then we were installed as Knights with the customary rites, and among other privileges set over Ignorance, Poverty, and Sickness, to deal with them as we wished. This was afterwards ratified in a little chapel, to which we were led in procession, and we gave thanks to God for it. Then I hung up my Golden Fleece and my hat in God's honor, and left them there as an everlasting memorial; and since each had to write his name, I wrote thus:

Summa scientia nihil scire.
Fr. CHRISTIANUS ROSENKREUTZ,
Eques aurei Lapidis:
Anno 1459.

[The height of knowledge is to know nothing. Brother Christian Rosenkreutz, Knight of the Golden Stone. In the year 1459.]

Others wrote otherwise, each as he saw fit. Then we were brought back into the hall and sat down, and were advised that we should consider quickly what we were going to wish for. The King and his party had gone into the little closet to hear our wishes themselves. Each one was called in there separately, so that I can say nothing about anyone else's wish. I had been thinking that nothing would be more laudable than to display some praiseworthy virtue for the honor of my Order, and now I could find none more honorable, or more hard-won, than Gratitude. Hence, although I could gladly have wished for something I desired more, I mastered myself and decided, whatever the danger, to release my benefactor the porter.

When I was called in, I was first asked, since I had read the petition, whether I had noticed or suspected anything about the culprit. Thereupon I fearlessly began to relate all the events that had passed, and how I had fallen into them through ignorance, and offered to atone for all I had done. The King and the other lords were much surprised at this unexpected news, and told me to step out for a while. As soon as I returned, Atlas informed me how painful it was to His Majesty that I, beloved by him above all, should have come to such misfortune; but that since they could not contravene their ancient traditions, nothing could prevent the porter from being freed, and myself put in his place. They hoped that another would soon be caught, so that I could go home again, but no release could be expected before the wedding-feast of the King's future son.

This verdict nearly killed me, and I was immediately furious with myself and my blabbing mouth for not keeping quiet. But in the end I took heart, and since it seemed unavoidable I related how this porter had given me a token and recommended me to the second porter, by whose help I resisted the scales and partook of all the honor and joy I had received. Since it was only right to be grateful to one's benefactor, and as it could not be otherwise, I accepted my sentence, and was happy to accept some inconvenience that would help him in his situation. But if something could still be done with my wish, I wished myself back home; thus he would be freed by me, and I by my wish.

They answered that wishes did not stretch as far as that, or else I could have simply wished him free. His Majesty was pleased that I had behaved so well, but was afraid that I did not yet realize what a sad condition my inquisitiveness had plunged me into. Now the good man was set at liberty, and I had to take my leave with a heavy heart.

After me, the others were summoned in, and all came out happy, which was all the more painful to me since I imagined that I would have to spend the rest of my life beneath the gate. I wracked my brains over what I should do and how I should spend the time. At length I concluded that I was already old, and had only a few more years to live; this misery and melancholy would soon do away with me, and then I would be done with gatekeeping. I could even bring myself into the grave by means of a peaceful sleep. I had many such thoughts. At times I was vexed that I had seen such beautiful things, and must be deprived of them. At other times I was happy that before my end I had been admitted to every joy and not sent away shamefully. But this was the last and rudest shock I suffered.

As I meditated thus, the others made ready, and after they had bade the King and Queen good night, each was conducted to his lodging. But no one showed me the way, and I, poor fellow, had to continue in my chagrin; also, to be in no doubt of my future function, I had to put on the ring that the other had worn before me. At last the King advised me that since this was now the last time I would see him in this condition, I should conduct myself according to my position, and not against the rules of the Order. Thereupon he took me in my arms and kissed me. From all of this I understood that tomorrow I must sit by my gate. After they had all talked to me in friendship a little longer and given me their hands, they wished me God's protection, and I was led by the two old men (the gentleman of the Tower and Atlas) into a splendid bedroom where three beds stood, and each lay in one of them. There we spent almost two...

[About two pages in quarto are missing here, in which the Author, thinking that he must be a gatekeeper in the morning, returns home.]

THE END

Straßburg/

SIMPLEX SPES

PRUDENTIA FIRMA.

Gedruckt bey Conrad Scher/

Im Jahr/ M. DC. XVI.

Commentary
by Adam McLean

The Chemical Wedding of Christian Rosenkreutz is undoubtedly the most profound and intricate of the Hermetic allegories. It is not a dry, technical alchemical treatise but a good, exciting, well-paced story with a freshness and charm that allures and intrigues all who read it. Some esotericists become fascinated by its web of symbolism and try to tease out its hidden meaning; however, it poses those who seek to unravel its mysteries many troubling and deeply challenging questions:

In what sense do the events reflect a wedding? The ceremony at the center of the allegory is hardly that of a wedding but more like a funeral. What is the special contribution of Christian Rosenkreutz to these events? He seems rather to be an actor in a scripted ritual, obeying a set of instructions. So in what sense does he bring anything new to this set program of events?

What is the relationship between the Castle and the Tower? Why does the allegory need these seemingly separate realms?

The Chemical Wedding is often claimed as a document of an esoteric Christianity, but where is the Christian message? What is described seems more like an ancient 'mystery initiation' than a Christian religious experience.

Anyone who sensitively reads the Chemical Wedding will find many such questions arising in their souls. On reading the story our souls feel stimulated and enlivened by the atmosphere it evokes in us, but we find ourselves at the same time puzzled and made intellectually uneasy by the mysterious power of its allegory. Its hidden mystery seems always just one step beyond our comprehension. The more we puzzle over it and appear to clear up one point, another layer of mystery arises from our new understanding of the symbolism, and occludes its meaning even deeper. Many esotericists despair of ever grasping its inner content, but all who work with this allegory come to respect the profound and masterly achievement of the creator of this elegantly sculpted symbolic tale.

It may well be that the Chemical Wedding is not meant to be

understood, and that its esoteric task is to hold before us a symbolic mirror within which we can see our own inner transformations reflected. Only through working on our inner world will the allegorical transformations carved into the substance of the *Chemical Wedding* become relevant and significant to us. These will not be sensed by the static intellect, but only by the dynamic evolving forces of the soul in a state of inner transformation.

So to attempt a commentary or explanation of this enigmatic work may appear presumptuous, and some people may even react against any analysis that might appear to compromise or strip away any layers of its mystery. There are great dangers in commenting on the *Chemical Wedding*, as we note in looking at the work of previous writers, who have often revealed only their own lack of insight or narrowness of vision in their attempts. The *Chemical Wedding* can be a severe test for the esotericist.

Those who have attempted commentaries on the work have perhaps tried too hard to grasp its essence within their own system of ideas, and have ended up merely projecting their own opinions and prejudices onto the mass of symbolic material. I have already mentioned in the Introduction J. W. Montgomery's appalling attempt (*Cross and Crucible*, The Hague, 1973) at explaining the *Chemical Wedding* as a work of Lutheran orthodoxy.

Rudolf Steiner's essay, *Die Chymische Hochzeit des Christian Rosenkreutz* (Munich, 1917), is similarly limited and rather disappointing as he attempts to bring its symbolism into his own 'anthroposophical' system of ideas. He avoids many of the deeply puzzling aspects of the work, and instead labors various points about mysticism and occultism that seem hardly relevant to the *Chemical Wedding*. We note, as an example, his vague waffling on the important symbols encountered in the process undertaken in the Tower, which merits deeper consideration than he is able to give to it. He erroneously interprets the seven weights as 'the Seven Liberal Arts,' ignoring the text of the *Chemical Wedding* which makes them out as moral qualities such as the seven Virtues, rather than intellectual achievements. (Thus Christian Rosenkreutz is worried about seeming too proud, as the vice of 'pride is expressly set against the fourth weight.') All the later anthroposophical commentators slavishly follow Steiner's line and fail to pick up this point.

Margaret Bennell and Isabel Wyatt's *An Introductory Commentary on The Chymical Wedding of Christian Rosenkreutz* (Stroud, 1964) is uncompromisingly anthroposophical, and they diligently attack the allegory with a barrage of Steiner-derived terms. If one reads their commentary carefully one will find little insight into the substance of the *Chemical Wedding* itself, but merely an expression of certain prime anthroposophical ideas on the structure of the soul and spirit of humanity and its evolution in time.

A later commentator, Hans van der Stok, in his *Contemplations on the Chymical Wedding* (Camphill Press, 1981), goes too far, stretching the allegory beyond its elastic limits in his attempt to incorporate some of the more obscure anthroposophical ideas about the great Initiates—Buddha, Mani, Zarathustra—somehow involved with Christian Rosenkreutz in the events (unbeknown to the writer of the story, one feels certain!) in company with an unknowable initiate visible only to Steiner's clairvoyance called 'Skythianos.' Stok has to bend the text to suit his purpose, making one of the characters in the story, the First Porter, also one of the nine chosen Wedding Guests. Absurdly, after his ascent of the Tower with Rosenkreutz, this guest must rush back to the castle and appear in his porter's uniform, in time to greet the guests as they return in triumph from the Tower! (However, it may be that such a rewriting of the script would have been of interest to its original author!) The truth is that Stok has unfortunately too many 'Initiates' in his set of anthroposophical ideas to fit into the scheme of the *Chemical Wedding*, so he is not averse to a little surgical intervention. Such an attempt merely betrays Stok's slavish adherence to his preconceived scheme of portraying the *Chemical Wedding* as foreshadowing Rudolf Steiner's idiosyncratic views on Rosicrucianism.

Paul Allen, another anthroposophist, in his excellent *Christian Rosenkreutz Anthology* (New York: Rudolph Steiner Publications, 1968), takes the wisest (and easiest) course and merely adds some useful comments in the form of notes.

Even the great scholar Frances Yates was befuddled by the *Chemical Wedding*. In chapter V of *The Rosicrucian Enlightenment*, which she devotes to the work, she shows how certain historically documented events in the court of the Palatinate could have influenced the writer of the *Chemical Wedding*, and that the actions of the tale could well be located in Heidelberg Castle. In this chapter she states that "the culmination of the whole story, at the end of the Seventh Day, was the reception of the guests into the Order of the Golden Stone, after which they sailed away in their ships." She then goes on to describe certain pageant cars in the form of ships that were used at Heidelberg. I am afraid that the convolutions of the allegory here got the better of Dame Frances, for this is not what happens in the story at all, as we can see by rereading the Seventh Day. Although this misreading does not distract from her thesis in any way, it does illustrate just how difficult a text this is to try and push an interpretation upon.

So there are great dangers in working with such an elaborate, mysterious and respected esoteric document, in that it can bring out the egoism of the commentator, who smugly smiles inwardly to his or her self and says 'Now I have finally cracked its code and expounded its mysteries.' The deepest esoteric documents are subtly protected, so that such simplistic interpretations will quite obviously appear as merely ridiculous, reflecting badly on the reputation of the commentator rather than damaging the essence of the work itself.

I hope I can avoid making too much of a fool of myself in preparing this present commentary. I do so in order to encourage others to work with this allegory. To merely publish the text would not have been enough, and the commentary provides, I hope, an impetus to further research. I trust my readers will understand that it is not presented here as a final solution of the riddle to the text.

For this present commentary I have taken a different approach from that of the previously mentioned writers. I have no wish to incorporate the *Chemical Wedding* into a preconceived system of ideas. My method has been to tune in and empathize with the allegory, and to try to find the archetypal shapes in which the symbols have been carved and fashioned. Rather than projecting an external net of ideas upon the text, I have tried to allow the inner structure of the *Chemical Wedding* to unfold itself. In working with the text for publication, I came to believe it needed a commentary because many people today find Hermetic symbols and allegories difficult to work with. Through my years of study, contemplation, and meditation upon such material, I perhaps am able to empathize with its structure, and hopefully can communicate some sense of its inner form to my readers. I have tried to allow my inner world to become like a mirror—catching the essence of the tale, reflecting its forms, and allowing its symbols to speak through my words. I hope readers will not judge me too harshly or hold that I have in any way attempted to reduce the *Chemical Wedding* to a simplistic interpretation suiting my own purposes. I have at all times tried to hold before me a sense of its mystery, and the breadth and scope of its symbols.

In my work with the *Chemical Wedding* I did have a sense of working with a living being. It has an inner vitality, a spark of inner life, that we must recognize and respect. Anyone who seeks to work with this allegory merely as a mine of symbolic substance to be molded to suit their own values and ideas will fail to touch upon its inner spark. As I worked with this in meditation over a period of some years, I have become aware that the *Chemical Wedding* still possesses an inner life force, and can still touch our souls with a living flame. I write this commentary in the hope that I might encourage others similarly to make a connection with the living force of soul transformation that lies in the kernel of the *Chemical Wedding of Christian Rosenkreutz*.

There were two main options open to me in writing this commentary. Either I could pursue the story sequentially, commenting upon each event as it unfolded and trying to illustrate its inner significance, or I could attempt to give an overall view of the basic symbolic structure of the allegory, so that we might come to see each aspect as part of the total process of transformation outlined in the story. I chose to take the latter course, as I felt it suited the multi-layered material of the allegory. Thus in no sense does this commentary attempt a summary of the *Chemical Wedding*.

Consequently readers will have to acquaint themselves with the tale in some detail if they are to be able to work with this commentary, which is certainly no substitute for reading the text.

In the first part of this commentary, I will look at and analyze in some depth certain important facets of the symbolism of the *Chemical Wedding*, while in the second half I will attempt to synthesize and show ways in which these symbols are echoed and reflected in different parts of the tale, in order that we might gain a picture of the process of inner transformation that is woven into this greatest of all alchemical allegories.

In this first section we will look at:

1) The Sevenfold Architecture of the Allegory
2) The Outer World, the Castle, and the Tower
3) The Characters in the Allegory
4) The Sight of Venus
5) The Altar
6) The Seven Gifts Bestowed and Received by Christian Rosenkreutz
7) The Dreams or Evening Experiences of Christian Rosenkreutz
8) The Fountain in the Garden and the Vessel in the Sepulcher of Venus
9) The Play within the Play
10) Venus, the Sirens' Song, and the Theme of Love
11) The Ascent of the Tower

And to conclude the commentary we will consider:

12) Working further with the *Chemical Wedding*
13) The Links with Goethe's *Fairy Tale of the Green Snake and the Beautiful Lily*
14) The Links with the *Parabola* of Hinricus Madathanus
15) Conclusion

The Sevenfold Architecture of the Allegory

A mere cursory reading will convince us that the fundamental symbolic architecture of this allegory is sevenfold. We can find many examples of this structure, though there are more subtle and less obvious sevenfold forms to be found, and an awareness of this will throw light upon the symbolic links between different parts of the allegory.

Among the obvious examples, the seven days during which the events of the *Chemical Wedding* take place provide a sure sevenfold foundation, and the short Comedy at the center of the tale which takes place in the middle of the Fourth Day has seven acts. This little 'play within a play' gives us a simple allegory which can help to unlock the greater allegory of the *Chemical Wedding*, and we will follow this up in detail later. Further, during the Fourth Day we find a sevenfold Altar (the black altar and six ritual objects), which also sets an important constellation of symbols, an understanding of which is essential to grasping the whole allegorical picture. We will examine this point in detail later.

On the First Day, during Rosenkreutz's dream of his imprisonment in the dungeon, the rope through which he can escape is let down seven times only. On the Sixth Day, he and his companions perform an alchemical operation which involves the ascent of the seven floors of the Tower of Olympus. These two are thus reflections of each other on different levels, as both involve ascending upwards through trap doors in the ceiling to freedom on a higher level. In the first (dream experience), this occurs through grace from the Matron above, but in the second (waking experience), it must be earned by the work of the operators on each level. Seven ships bear the company to the Tower, and there are seven verses in the Sirens' song to them during this journey. The weighing ceremony of the Third Day uses seven weights against which to test the guests.

These are only some of the more obvious sevenfold elements. The reader will find it of the greatest value to look for other sevenfold symbolism that may be buried a little deeper in the text.

On the First Day, Christian Rosencreutz receives a letter bearing the Hieroglyphic Monad. This has in fact seven symbolic elements composing its complex form ☿ : Moon crescent ☽, solar circle ⊙, central dot or point •, vertical bar of Cross |, and its horizontal bar ——, a left crescent ⌒ and a right crescent ⌒. John Dee analyzes his symbol in this way in his book on the Hieroglyphic Monad published in 1564. So when Rosenkreutz receives this symbol it is an indication to him that the work will indeed be sevenfold.

Rosenkreutz passes through seven tests:

The test of the Letter	whether he has the courage to go or not
The test of the Four Ways	gives up bread, uses qualities of balance, the compass
The test of the First Portal	gives up his water
The test of the Second Portal	gives up his salt
The test of the Third Portal	gives up his outer garments
The test of the Hall of Guests	elects to stay behind, humility
The test of the Weighing	the scales

Rosenkreutz has seven things with him on the journey which he has to give away at various stages. He also receives seven tokens or medals. I will describe these in detail in a separate section.

The Ceremony of the Weighing tests each guest against seven weights. These are obviously the Seven Virtues (not the Seven Liberal Arts, as Steiner and the anthroposophists seem determined to have us believe—the whole tone of this part of the allegory is the testing of the moral development of the guests, not of their grasp of Grammar, Rhetoric, Dialectic, etc.). The weights are described as being four small ones (these could be the four Moral or Cardinal Virtues of Wisdom, Justice, Temperance, and Fortitude), two larger ones (Faith and Hope, probably) with Love as the single large weight (it is this weight that the first Emperor fails to raise). There are few clues as to precisely how these are ascribed to the weights. It is interesting that Rosenkreutz outlines the total numbers of guests who raised each number of weights as follows:

7	raised	1	weight
21	raised	2	weights
35	raised	3	weights
35	raised	4	weights
21	raised	5	weights
7	raised	6	weights

We note that these are the precise total of possible mathematical combinations of seven qualities taken 1, 2, 3, 4, 5 and 6 at a time. The guests therefore represent all the possible states of human virtue.

Towards the end of the Third Day, seven riddles are exchanged between the maidens and the men who had been successful at the weighing.

On the Fourth Day shortly before the wedding, the maidens play a trick upon the men by forming the company into a ring and suggesting that each seventh one, counting round the circle, shall partner and sleep with the next. This is a cunning device, for they have arranged themselves so that on counting, the maidens are partnered only with maidens and the men are left standing alone. The pattern they adopted was probably as illustrated.

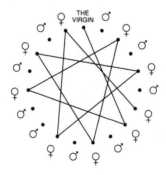

The 'Wedding' ceremony involves the beheading of seven people—the Bride and Bridegroom, the two ancient Kings and their Queens, together with the Moor who performs the execution. Through the death of these seven, their essence is gathered into nourishing the 'Bird' which the operators work with in the Tower on the Sixth Day, from which are reborn the new King and Queen.

The Castle of the Bridegroom has seven rooms, halls or regions into which Christian Rosenkreutz is admitted:

1) the realm of the Outer Gates, and the Ante-chamber in which he is tonsured
2) the Dining Hall in which he meets the other guests, and which is used as the Hall of the Weighing
3) the Garden in which the sentences are passed on the guests, and which is later the place of the mock-burial of the bodies of the Bride and Groom
4) the Library and the room of the Great Globe
5) the royal winding stairs leading to the Hall of the Wedding
6) the House of the Sun, to which the party proceed to see the Comedy performed
7) the underground Chamber of Venus

Thus the *Chemical Wedding* has many sevenfold processes worked into its complex symbolism. The most obvious of these is, of course, the fact that its events take place over a period of seven days. Esotericists will be excused for immediately seeking a 'planetary' interpretation of these sevenfold processes; however, if we attempt this we will find such an association rather unproductive of insights. Something else seems to be working here. Although there are undoubted parallels with planetary archetypes, if we let the symbolism of the *Chemical Wedding* reveal itself and its inner patterns and energies rather than trying to force it into a 'planetary' mold, as it were, we will find a more significant sevenfold process working within the symbols.

These seven stages, found in the overall plan of the seven days, in the ascent of the Tower, in the Comedy and in various other processes in the allegory, can be characterized in the following way. The Seven divides into three phases—an initial threefold group, a central single stage, and a concluding threefold grouping. This whole archetypal process outlines the formation, the coming into incarnation, and the outer expression of a spiritual impulse. Thus we have three initial stages during which a spiritual impulse is initiated and shaped; a single central stage where it meets and fuses with its embodiment, which is a period of the earthing of this impulse; and a final triplicity of stages for the expression of the impulse from this center into outer forms. In this sense, we have an involutionary arc (a central period of epigenesis) and a final evolutionary phase; or in other terms, an impress of the spiritual into incarnation (a centering or earthing) and an excarnatory phase of expression.

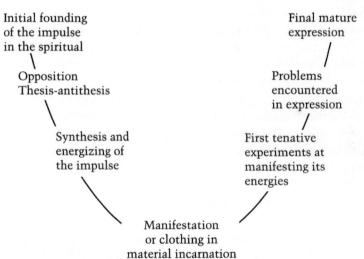

INVOLUTIONARY ARC   EVOLUTIONARY ARC

Initial founding   Final mature
of the impulse   expression
in the spiritual

Opposition   Problems
Thesis-antithesis   encountered
                                                      in expression

Synthesis and   First tenative
energizing of   experiments at
the impulse   manifesting its
                                                      energies

                    Manifestation
                    or clothing in
                 material incarnation

The first stage of the initial phase is a pure experience of the essence of the impulse, a unitary vision of a spiritual form. The next stage is the experience of a kind of crisis, where this impulse meets a dualistic opposition. The third and last stage of this initial phase of the process is where the thesis and antithesis of the second stage are able to come together into a new synthesis. This birth of a third balancing facet gives rise to a focusing of the potential energy of the second stage and a consequent dynamic energizing of the initial impulse.

The central stage (the fourth) of this archetypal sevenfold transformation process is the turning point where the initial spiritual impulse, having overcome its opposition and become energized, ties itself into incarnation, and through focusing itself in a single point, event, or individual act, penetrates into its lowest vehicle, and enfolds its being into actualization through an inner transformation of essence into substance.

Then arises the upward arc of the three phases expressing this inner spiritual impulse in outer manifestation. The first stage of this group (the fifth in the total cycle) sees the raw expression of the energy of this impulse. Here, although it is as yet unintegrated and lacks form, it is nevertheless able to pour its energies into outer manifestation. These tentative explorations of its new power are tempered by its interaction with the real world. The next stage is a crisis—corresponding to and mirroring that of the second stage— in which the expression of this new impulse meets opposition and material antithesis, and a check to its manifestation. These it must inwardly and outwardly overcome through synthesizing this thesis-antithesis into a new unity. This unity constitutes the seventh and final stage of the process, where the spiritual impulse, initially remote in the subtle realm of the spirit during its first stage, has through descending into manifestation been able to clothe itself in materiality while retaining its essence. The wholeness of this essence comes full circle to a mature expression in this seventh stage.

This archetypal sevenfold pattern is in fact one of the secrets of alchemy, one of the skeleton frameworks upon which the alchemists hung their symbols.

We should be able to recognize this structure underlying any process in which we try to bring an initial inspiration into manifestation. Indeed, in a sense, we can find these rhythms in the cycle of our weekly work. For ideally we should begin each week with a sense of a new impulse seeking manifestation through our efforts, and as the week unfolds, experience the oppositions, energies, and unfolding of the seven stages as we try to bring our creative impulse to an outer expression.

Seen from the side of matter, from the domain of manifestation, this is a descent of a new impulse from above and its meeting with, and embodiment in, that which is below, with the consequent enlivening and inspiration that gives rise to a new expression of its spiritual power.

Seen from the domain of spirit, this is a descent or death of an impulse that lived in the spirit, but if this process is successful then it is experienced as a resurrection or rebirth. This is, I believe, the central motif of the *Chemical Wedding*, and is subtly hinted at in the opening sentence which shows that the events begin on Easter Eve, the Saturday evening upon which symbolically the Christ or divine spiritual impulse died and descended deep into the earth in order to be resurrected and reborn.

The seven days of the *Chemical Wedding* work according to this archetypal form. On the First Day, Christian Rosenkreutz receives the spiritual impulse to attend the wedding (in the form of the letter of invitation delivered by the Angel-Virgin). On the Second Day, he experiences various oppositions to his journey. Though initially all seems well he soon has to encounter antitheses to his wish to attend the wedding (his choice of the four ways, passing the guardians or porters at the gates). However, he overcomes all these tests and early on the Third Day is given a new energy and impetus through his success on the scales. Later, he receives new insights from exploring the realm of the Castle.

On the Fourth Day, Rosenkreutz has to witness the outward presentation of the wedding ceremony. He has to see the black Altar, attend the Comedy, and witness the bloody wedding-execution. This is the turning point of the whole cycle. After this deeply moving experience has woven the essence of the wedding ritual into his soul, Rosenkreutz has to begin to manifest these energies.

Thus on Day Five he feels confident enough to explore regions of the Castle previously barred and hidden from him. The company have to go on a voyage to the realm of the Tower in order to manifest the evolutionary arc of the work. On the Sixth Day, the alchemists have to struggle to bring their work into expression, and experience the difficulties with the ladders, ropes, and wings in ascending the Tower, and in achieving success in their work at each stage. Significantly, the allegory puts a special difficulty or seeming opposition before Christian Rosenkreutz and the three more advanced adepts, as they prepare to move from the sixth to the seventh level. Here, through a trick they are made to feel that they have failed to give expression to their understanding of the process. The Seventh Day is the final mature expression of the work, and here Christian Rosenkreutz has to face up to his own responsibility for the process and takes on the role of guardian or porter of the first gate.

So we see how the seven days of the *Chemical Wedding* reflect this archetypal sevenfold pattern of transformation, rather than a simplistic 'planetary' scheme. If we center the process on the young King or Bridegroom, we see that he has to die on the Fourth Day, and in order for this act to take place he must have gathered to himself a group of adepts whom he can make responsible for his resurrection. Thus the first three days of his involutionary arc gathers together and tests this group of adepts from the outer world, while his evolutionary arc requires a visit to the realm of the Tower in order to effect his resurrection. We will again follow this sevenfold pattern when we look in detail at the Comedy and the Process undertaken in the Tower.

Each of the seven days seems to have a sevenfold structure, and can be without any artificiality subdivided into seven separate acts or linked events. It is interesting to try to analyze the actions of each day against the archetypal sevenfold pattern.

The First Day	Rosenkreutz in meditation
	appearance of the 'Angel of the Annunciation'
	sees Letter of invitation
	feels inadequate, does not know what to do
	dream
	sense of positivity
	prepares himself for the journey
The Second Day	The four ways
	first Porter

second Porter
third Porter
with the guests in the hall
bound and left in the hall
dream

The Third Day   weighing ceremony
scene in the dining hall
the passing of the sentences in the garden
visits the library and the great globe
the riddles in the hall
the Queen or Duchess and the hanging up of the
   weights dream

The Fourth Day   drinks of the fountain
meets the King and Queen
the 'bedfellows' trick of the maidens
procession to and performance of the play
the promise before the altar
wedding-execution
sees soul-flames over the lake

The Fifth Day   Rosenkreutz sees Venus unveiled
the mock burial in the Garden
company embarks on seven ships across the
   great lake
the Sirens' song
arrival at the Tower of Olympus
work in the first-level laboratory
vision of planetary conjunction and soul flames

The Sixth Day   the six further levels of the Tower
and the scene with the Warder at the end of
   the day

The Seventh Day   given 'Knights of the Golden Stone' medal
company embarks on twelve ships
meets with King and Queen and procession to

The Seventh Day	Castle
(continued)	King consults advisors about the Venus incident
	ceremonially installed as 'Knights of the Golden Stone'
	Christian Rosenkreutz admits to having seen Venus
	Rosenkreutz, Warder of the Tower, and Atlas meet

The Outer World, the Castle, and the Tower

There are three separate realms which are brought through the action of the allegory into a new relationship: The outer world, the everyday realm of material embodiment, where we first meet Christian Rosenkreutz in his chamber and to which he returns at the end of the story; the realm of the Castle of the Bridegroom; and the island fortress of the Tower of Olympus, to which they have to journey in order to bring about the transformation and resurrection.

These realms are initially cut off from each other, but somehow need each other. Thus the wedding in the Castle of the Bridegroom needs people from the outer world in order that its strange ritual can be successful. These people must be sufficiently morally and spiritually developed, so difficulties are put in their path and they have to be tested by a 'soul' weighing ceremony. The wedding ceremony in the Castle, which takes the form of a funeral, needs the journey to the realm of the Tower of transformation in order to heal and resurrect the Bride and Groom. Thus the Castle is dependent both on the realm of the Tower for the full experience and completion of its *Chemical Wedding*, and on the outer world from which it needs the help of such as Christian Rosenkreutz and his colleagues in witnessing and performing this ritual of resurrection.

In the outer world, Christian Rosenkreutz is a Brother of the Red-Rosie Cross, while in the domain of the Castle he becomes a Knight of the Golden Fleece, and later, after the successful ascent of the Tower, he is made a Knight of the Golden Stone. Thus he undergoes three levels of initiation, each corresponding to one of the three domains of the allegory.

He has to enter his name in three books. The first is put before him at the third gate on the threshold of the Castle. He has to sign his name, and we can suppose that he also entered his title as Brother of the Red-Rosie Cross into this book. The next book is that black volume which lay on the altar. Just before the wedding-execution, the Bridegroom makes the company of adepts promise to stay and help him in his imminent adversity, appealing to their honor as Knights of the Golden Fleece. After the work has been successfully performed, the adepts are all raised to the status of Knights of the Golden Stone and have to enter their names in a third book. Christian Rosenkreutz signs himself there as follows:

> The height of knowledge is to know nothing.
> Brother Christian Rosenkreutz,
> Knight of the Golden Stone.
> In the year 1459.

The Characters in the Allegory

Although the *Chemical Wedding* is long and elaborate, with many complex themes, the main characters in the action seem to have been pared down to an absolute minimum. We can identify seven main characters who have a primary part to play in the action:

Christian Rosenkreutz
The First Porter
The Virgin
The Old Queen or Duchess
The Bridegroom
Old Atlas, the court astromomer and counsellor
The Old Gentleman, Warder of the Tower of Olympus

Then there are a number of minor characters, who have an entirely subordinate or passive role in the proceedings:

The Virgin-messenger, who brings the wedding invitation
The Second Porter
The Third Porter
The maidens, attendants to the Virgin
The pages
The Captains and soldiery
The Bride
The Old Kings and their Queens
The Moor
The First Emperor
Rosenkreutz' companion and friend
Sirens
Lady Venus
Cupid

Let us look at some of the relationships between the characters.

Christian Rosenkreutz and the Young King or Bridegroom

These are the only two figures in the allegory in whom any inner change seems to take place. So the destinies of these two main figures are intimately tied together. The Bridegroom's resurrection is dependent on the work of Rosenkreutz, and Rosenkreutz' spiritual development and elevation to the Order of the Golden Stone is dependent in turn on his being invited to the wedding ceremony. The Bridegroom-King refers on Day Seven to Rosenkreutz as being 'his father.' This is true in a spiritual sense, for only through the diligent work of Rosenkreutz is he able to be reborn.

Christian Rosenkreutz and the Virgin

Although the relationship between the Bridegroom and our hero may constitute the esoteric core of the work, it is the relationship of Rosenkreutz to the Virgin which provides much of the entertainment and brings liveliness and sparkle to the action. The Virgin is a fascinating and important character. Whenever she appears in the story, we can be sure that some interesting events are about to unfold. She appears to be playing out a role, acting a scripted ritual; one does not have any sense of her own inner evolution or development as a being. She is, nevertheless, the main representative of the authority of the Castle, having an essential role as its steward, organizer of the rituals, and entertainer of the guests. During Days Three to Six, the male contingent of the Castle seem rather powerless figures lurking passively in the background, while the Virgin provides the impulse to all the action, being in a sense their agent. This state of affairs continues until the Seventh Day; then, when the work is completed, the Virgin retreats into the background and the male figures of the King, Old Atlas and the Porter dominate the scene and reassert their authority.

It is fascinating to picture this bright, charming, subtle, witty and wise Virgin as she leads us through the action at a fairly brisk pace, teasing the men and thoroughly enjoying the role she plays with them. Without her, the *Chemical Wedding* would be a terribly dry affair, and the creation of her character certainly was an act of genius on the part of its author. She seems so lively and rounded as a personality that she along with Christian Rosenkreutz are perhaps the only figures in the work one can think of as real persons— all the others can only be seen as archetypes.

On the Fourth Day, Christian Rosenkreutz is bold enough to ask her name, and she answers with a riddle, the solution to which is ALCHYMIA.

1st letter	1	=	A
2nd letter	12	=	L
3rd letter	3	=	C
4th letter	8	=	H
5th letter	9	=	I
6th letter	13	=	M
7th letter	9	=	I
8th letter	1	=	A
	56		

The solution to this riddle was first proposed by the philosopher Leibniz, who was very interested in Rosicrucianism.

The First Porter and Christian Rosenkreutz
These two share a special secret or destiny in that they have both gazed upon the 'sleeping Venus' immured in a chamber beneath the

Castle. The inhabitants of the Castle seem unable to make a positive relationship with the powerful elemental forces of the feminine, and in their pursuit of a lofty, abstract science and remote religion have attempted to seal up this feminine element, the archetypal Venus, in the depths of their Castle. Because Christian Rosenkreutz penetrated this secret, he must of necessity take on the role of First Porter. Only those who are aware of what the castle keeps hidden and sealed up in its Royal Treasury can take on the role of Guardian of the First Gate, for only they can recognize those who are worthy in turn to discover this inner secret.

Old Atlas, the Warder of the Tower, and Christian Rosenkreutz

These three are seen to have a special relationship: during the evening of the Seventh Day after the work is completed, they retire together to a chamber in the Castle. Old Atlas is astrologer and advisor to the King, and in this sense he is the 'Wise Man of the Realm of the Castle.' The Warder is, of course, the 'Wise Man of the Realm of the Tower,' and Christian Rosenkreutz can be seen as the 'Wise Man or Initiate from the Outer World.' When these three meet together in the Brotherhood they unite the wisdom of the three realms.

The Old Queen, the Virgin, and the Bride

The old Queen (also referred to as the 'Duchess' in marginal notes to the Foxcroft translation) and the Virgin are the two most important female archetypal figures actively involved in the story.

This old Queen, whom we first meet towards the close of the Third Day, seems to have her whole demeanor turned heavenwards, and seeks the spiritual through a pious religous devotion. She is unworldly, remote and, one feels, rather unctuous and puritanical, her own room being furnished only with a pulpit and prayer books. She wastes no time in telling Christian Rosenkreutz, with all the tones of a Protestant sermon: "You have received more than the others; see that you also give more!" On the Fourth Day she leads the stately procession from the King's Hall to the House of the Sun, bearing before her a crucifix. She also rides in the procession on the Seventh Day from the shore of the lake to the

Castle. She should not be confused with the other queens who are beheaded with their husbands on the fourth day. She is obviously not on the same level as the other queens in the allegory and has a relatively small part to play in the action. Perhaps she is there to reflect an opposite to the worldly, witty Virgin, who is given to more earthly ribaldry. However, in this process it is the Virgin who has the more active part in the work, though she does adopt a subservient role towards the old Queen at the Ceremony of the Hanging-Up of the Weights late on the Third Day. The old Queen and the Virgin seem worlds apart, immersed in different realms.

If we see this old Queen as symbolically representing the feminine forces of the soul given up to and immersed in a heavenly devotion and renunciation of the world, and the Virgin as these forces seeking spiritual fulfilment through the channel of the earthly world, then the one female figure who has to strive to unite these two within herself must surely be the Bride. Although the *Chemical Wedding* does not attempt to give the character of the Bride any real substance, as the wife of the King we see that she is put in the position of having to balance the heavenly against the earthly. Interestingly, almost the only picture we have of her outside a merely ceremonial role is on the Seventh Day, where she plays a kind of chess with the King in which virtues and vices are pitted against each other.

In a Castle where the male domination has sealed up the primal energies of the Venus forces deep in an underground vault, the old Queen represents the King's direct experience of the feminine. The old Queen is the heavenward-turning, devotional, world-renouncing, and nun-like aspect of the feminine in the court, while the Virgin reflects the earthly and worldly side of the feminine there. The Lutheran apologist Montgomery may have touched upon a true perception when he followed Rudolf Steiner in identifying the old Queen as 'Theologia' complementing the Virgin as 'Alchimia.' The task of Theology is surely to bring humanity to an awareness of the Spirit through an upward gaze and renunciation of the world, whereas Alchimia is the sacred science of transformation that does not require a rejection of the path of the earthly realm. These two are the complementary facets of Sophia. Montgomery is regrettably unable to recognize the need for both of these polarities, and instead interprets the intention of the author of the *Chemical Wedding* as elevating the 'Duchess Theologia' above the merely worldly 'Virgin Alchimia.'

The Emperor and Rosenkreutz' Friend

These two seem to be antitheses of each other. Rosenkreutz' friend or companion whom he meets in the Castle, "a quiet and refined man," is an ideal fellow adept, who behaves himself impeccably throughout the story. Indeed, he accompanies Rosenkreutz on an exploration of the library and monuments of the Castle, and sits with him in the interior of the great globe. The Emperor, on the other hand, is quite unworthy of the trust which Rosenkreutz puts in him. For although it was Rosenkreutz who released him when he failed on the scales, nevertheless, just before the sentences are passed on the other guests who were not so honored, this ungrateful Emperor behaves so abominably towards him in a way that Rosenkreutz cannot tell, "for fear of malicious gossip." Interestingly, it is the Emperor, together with Rosenkreutz and his friend, who are instrumental in determining the sentences passed on the failed guests.

The Sight of Venus

On the morning of the Fifth Day, Christian Rosenkreutz descends in the company of his page into the underground chamber beneath the castle and intrudes into regions the Royal Persons would not have him see. This realm was called the King's Treasury, and beyond it, barred by an iron door with copper letters, was a chamber in which lay Lady Venus. The castle above is full of wondrous inventions. Its valued possessions are subtle mechanical devices, such as the great globe of the world, and other works of science and the creative intellect. However, deep in the foundations of the Castle, well hidden from all eyes, lies Lady Venus locked up, unable to manifest her forces, for she is in a state of suspended animation or coma, in an underground chamber having all the qualities of a mausoleum. (Indeed, the page tells Rosenkreutz that the coffins bearing the royal bodies from the 'Wedding' had earlier been stored in this underground vault.)

The Castle is outwardly dedicated to lofty abstractions, the pursuit of the Arts and Sciences, and is only able to achieve this through an unbalanced, one-sided development of the forces of the human soul; it needs to deny and hide away under lock and key the primal Venus forces in the soul, the powerful passions of the feminine side of human nature. (The text subtly underlines this point by having the door of the vault of Venus made of Iron, the hard masculine Mars metal, while the letters that tell that she lies within are of Copper, the softer Venus metal.) Because of this distorted polarization—this fear of the masculine powers in the realm of the Castle of being engulfed by the powerful feminine energies—any meeting between the masculine and feminine must result in inner struggle and death. Thus the wedding of the King and Queen can only be achieved in this Castle through a death process. The masculine abstract, scientific, and artistic crafts of the realm of the Castle have been bought at a high price.

The strange copper letters on the door of the vault (see the Fifth Day) are in fact a simple substitution code first solved by Seelander in 1736.

a - x	b - ƌ	c - ɔs	d - 6	e - ppȣ
f - ʃ	g - ǥ	h - bh	i - 2ʃ[-y?]	k - ƙ,ʄ
l - 8	m - ȯ	n - ö	o - ȯ	r - s
s - ƀs	t - ǥ	u - o	w - ω	z - ȥ

These spell out in German *Hye lygt begraben / Venus, / dye schön Fraw, so manchen / Hoen man / umb glück, ehr, segen, und wolfart / gebracht hatt*, which, in fact, appears in full in the text a few lines further down the page. In English it reads, "Here lies buried Venus, the fair woman who has undone many a great man in fortune, honor, blessing, and prosperity."

This also applies to the lettering on the tablet beside the sleeping Venus, which decodes easily into German as *Wan dye Frutcht meynes baums wyrt vollends verschmelzen, werde ych aufwachen und eyn muter seyn eynes konygs,* which appears a few lines later in the text. In English this says, "When the fruit of my tree has completely melted, I shall awake and be the mother of a King."

So although this cipher writing might seem at first sight to hide some special secret or key to the allegory of the *Chemical Wedding,* it is merely a blind or mystification as the message is spelled out in the text.

The Altar

The altar which Christian Rosenkreutz sees on the Fourth Day when he meets the King and Queen in their Hall provides a constellation of symbols important in the process of transformation. This altar also appears on the sixth level of the Tower and all its sacred objects are ritually used there in the sacrifice of the Bird.

This altar has six objects upon it:

   a book covered in black velvet, outlined with gold
   an ever-burning taper in a candlestick
   a sphere or globe revolving by itself
   a small striking clock
   an ever-flowing fountain
   a skull or death's head with a serpent eternally circling
      through the eye holes

Apart from the book, the other five objects share the common property of having a self-sustaining, inward-driving force: the ever-burning taper, the globe turning by itself, the clock striking by itself, the ever-flowing fountain, the continually circling snake in the skull.

Immediately before the wedding-execution, Christian Rosenkreutz and his colleagues note how the lamps in the Hall are lit at the ever-burning taper (to which Cupid pays great attention and occasionally blows upon to make sure that it is still alight). They are asked to pledge themselves to the resurrection of the King, write their promise in the black Book, and take a 'draught of silence' from the ever-flowing fountain. We also note that the King is especially concerned that the serpent is well fed, as his future resurrection depends on the blood of this serpent, as we see on the sixth level of the Tower.

In the Tower, the altar is set up on the sixth floor, and all its objects are used in the sacrifice of the Bird. The bird drinks of the fountain, then pecks at the serpent, and the operators take the serpent's blood and feed it to the Bird. They wait until the watch strikes three times and the globe turns to a third special conjunction, whereupon the Bird lays its head upon the black Book and is beheaded. Its body is then burnt to ashes by a fire kindled at the ever-burning taper.

The ritual objects on this altar are all eternally renewing themselves or recycling without end, and this is one reason why the King can trust in the ritual for his resurrection. Rosenkreutz and his companions must enter their names into the Book, promising faithfully to carry out this ritual of resurrection.

Seven Gifts Bestowed and Received by Christian Rosenkreutz

Rosenkreutz has seven things with him on the journey which he has to give away at various stages—his Bread, Water and Salt, his outer garments (coat and shoes), his hair, his four roses, and his hat. The Bread he gives away to the Dove during the test of the ways, while his bottle of Water and his Salt he bestows as gifts to the First and Second Porters. His coat he has to leave behind trapped in the Third Gate, where he is also called upon to give away his shoes to an old man by this gate. Before he enters the Hall of the Castle, he has to submit to tonsure and loses the hair from the crown of his head to some invisible barbers. The sixth thing he has to give away are the four roses which he placed in his hat when he set out upon his journey to the wedding. These he bestows on the Virgin after he has been successful at the weighing ceremony of the Third Day. Finally, he hangs up his hat together with the Golden Fleece he received as a gift on the fourth day, in the Chapel of the Knights of the Golden Stone.

He receives seven gifts or tokens during the space of the wedding:

On the First Day, during his dream, he receives from the Matron who rescued him from the dungeon a token of gold with a rising sun stamped on the one side and the letters D.L.S. on the other. (The notes at this point have the following possible interpretations: Deus Lux Solis "God, the light of the sun," Deo Laus Semper "Praise always to God.")

On the Second Day he receives a special token from the First Porter, which, as is revealed later, helps him in the weighing ceremony to withstand the seven weights. This golden token has the letters S.C. upon it. (The notes here suggest: Sanctitate Constantia "Constant in holiness," or Sponsus Charus "Beloved husband," or Spes Charitas "Hope, charity.")

At the next gate, the Second Porter gives him a further token with the letters S.M. upon it. (The marginalia here suggest: Studio Merentis "By studying the worthy," Sal Humor "Humor salt," Sponso Mittendus "Pledge for the Bridegroom," Sal Mineralis "Mineral Salt," Sal Menstrualis "Menstrual Salt.")

At the Third gate he receives yet another token, this time with the letters S.P.N. This is referred to as "the proper guest-token," and the marginalia interpret the letters as Salus per Naturam "Salvation through Nature," or Sponsi praesentandus Nuptiis "To be presented to the Bridegroom at the wedding."

The fifth token, which he receives on the Third Day just after the weighing, is a medallion of the Golden Fleece with a flying lion presented on behalf of the Bridegroom.

The sixth token is given on the morning of the Fourth Day and is a grander Golden Fleece set about with precious stones. On it hangs a medal of gold, on one side of which are shown the sun and moon in opposition, while on the other is inscribed this short verse:

> The moon's light shall be like the sun's light, and the sun's light shall be seven times as bright.

On the morning of the Seventh Day, after their success in the process, the Virgin declares Christian Rosenkreutz and his colleagues to be Knights of the Golden Stone, and the old gentleman of the Tower presents each of them with a medal of gold, on one side of which is AR. NAT. MI. ("Art is the Minister of Nature") while on the other is TEM. NA. F. ("Nature is the daughter of Time").

The Dreams or Evening Experiences of Christian Rosenkreutz

At the end of each day Christian Rosenkreutz has a dream or experience which warns or enlightens him as to forthcoming events.

First evening	dream of the dungeon
Second evening	dream of people suspended from a height
Third evening	dream of a door he cannot open
Fourth evening	sees in full consciousness the bodies of the Royal persons being taken on board the seven ships, and also the flames or spirits of the departed.
Fifth evening	notes a rare and favorable conjunction of the planets, and sees in full consciousness seven spirit flames hovering above the Tower.
Sixth evening	sound of the sea lulls him to sleep; one peaceful dream occupies him all night
Seventh evening	text breaks off at this point

As the action of the allegory proceeds, both the length and significance of his dreams lessens. As Christian Rosenkreutz goes through the process he seems to become more conscious and does not need to receive spiritual insights through his dreams. It is significant that they occur only on the first three evenings. The first dream is the longest and most important as it helps him to understand that he has been chosen by grace to attend the wedding, and not to fear going on the journey. The dream of the second evening is a prefiguring of the fall of the proud at the weighing, and indeed it is his humility that makes him especially successful at the weighing. However, this dream occurs after he has chosen to stay in the hall, and so it does not influence him in the way that the first dream did, but rather confirms his decision to remain in the Hall.

The dream of the third evening is dismissed in one sentence and has little predictive power. We see quite clearly that during his attendance at the wedding, the power of his dream life lessens. This can be seen as an indication that, in entering the realm of the Castle, he is taking a conscious step into the astral or soul world.

After that, it is events perceived in full consciousness that are the source of the spiritual insights he receives in his night-time experiences. Thus on the fourth evening he sees the bodies being taken aboard the ships with the spirit flames departing over the lake. The fact that he has seen this enables him alone of all the company to understand why he must sail across the lake to the realm of the Tower and begin the process of transformation and rebirth.

On the fifth evening his perception of the special conjunction of the planets and the spirit-flames on the Tower aids him in grasping the process he will shortly have to undertake, especially that of the sixth level, where waiting for the right conjunction is very important to the resurrection process. Also, when he is on the seventh level he knows to look up to the roof of the Tower to see the soul-spirit flames descend into the bodies of the King and Queen. Since his companions did not share his experience of the night before, they are not aware of this descent of the spirits from above, and must think of the enlivening force coming into the manikins as arising from their work below.

The Fountain in the Garden and the Vessel in the Sepulcher of Venus

On the Third Day, just after the weighing ceremony, all of the unsuccessful guests are conducted to the Garden where sentence is to be passed upon them. Christian Rosenkreutz notes an impressive fountain bearing enigmatic letters. After the sentences have been carried out and the guests sent on their way, an atmosphere of peace descends on the Garden and there appears a beautiful snow-white Unicorn with a golden collar. This Unicorn comes forward and bows down on its front legs to the Lion who stands upon the top of the fountain. The Lion then breaks a sword it holds in its paws into pieces, which fall into the waters of the fountain, and begins roaring. Shortly afterward a Dove appears, bearing an olive branch which the Lion eats and is pacified. (This breaking of the sword corresponds to the conclusion of the sentencing, when the Virgin breaks her wand.) Christian Rosenkreutz and his companions have to purify themselves at this fountain, bathing their hands and heads in its waters. Later, on the morning of the Fourth Day, they are led to the fountain again and have to drink of its water (an inner purification to complete the outer one). They then see an inscription which indicates that this fountain contains a healing element.

This healing aspect seems to arise from the fountain uniting the polarities. The male forces of the Lion initially guard the fountain, the upwelling forces of the lower soul, but when he sees the Unicorn he is able to break his sword and be united with the essence of the feminine Dove. The Unicorn represents the fusion of the masculine and feminine, the solar and lunar aspects of the soul, being decidedly masculine and at the same time having a feminine lunar quality.

This fountain must be symbolically linked with the fountain-vessel in the Sepulcher of Venus. Here the vessel is triangular (made of copper, the Venus metal), and in the center stands an angel figure holding a tree. Through the heating of the sepulcher by the small tapers, the fruits of this tree melt and fall into the vessel, turning to a water which runs out through three channels into separate vessels, these three being associated with the three archetypal animal forms: the eagle, the ox and the lion. A tablet nearby indicates that when the tree is quite melted down, Lady Venus will awake and be the mother of a king.

So again we have a fountain of polarities. The tree is the symbol of this polarity, transforming through its roots the lower earthly realm below into the fruits on its branches in the higher realm above. This tree is held aloft by the angel (the human facet of the fourfold cosmic archetypes, lion-bull-eagle-man). If the human soul wishes to separate and distance itself from its animal side and, like an angel, hold aloft a tree of polarity, it can only do this by repressing and burying an important side of its nature, residing in the Venus forces. Thus, only when the tree is quite melted down and the dualistic tendencies of the human soul have been overcome will we be able to become consciously aware of the potentialities of the Venus realm within our souls: then symbolically Lady Venus will awake and bear a child, a new king. (Interestingly, during the process of transformation in the Tower, the Virgin discourses especially upon 'smelting.')

Although it is referred to in the text as an "unknown tree," we can be more than certain that our author intends parallels to the Garden of Eden story, and that this is the apple tree. Thus one way of looking at this sleeping Venus is as the fallen Eve of the Biblical account. The author of the *Chemical Wedding* seems to be asking us to reconsider what the human soul has lost through its adherence to the accepted religious dogma that made people reject the 'Eve facet' of their souls, seeing this aspect merely as a female temptress who leads the 'male facet' of their souls into 'evil trespass' and death. To the author of the *Chemical Wedding*, it was only by rediscovering, as does Rosenkreutz, the hidden realm of our souls symbolized in this Venus figure, and, at the same time, overcoming our dualistic view of our souls having a higher side that must repress the lower—a good facet that must hide away our evil sinful nature—that we can be inwardly transformed and spiritually reborn. It is the failure of the King of the Castle to come to terms with this aspect of his own being that leads him to ritualize an encounter (his wedding) with the feminine as a death process. In this sense, the King represents all of us in our present state of development, where we too have not yet been able to overcome these deep contradictions of our inner world. This Castle is truly the realm of the human soul, a place where all the characters have to struggle to develop and evolve the inner life of their souls.

The Lion facet of the first fountain can only overcome his need for the sword, his symbol of polarized masculine aggression, by his vision of the spiritual Unicorn which unites the polarities of its being so harmoniously and gracefully. In a similar way, the vessel in the Sepulcher of Venus will only become unpolarized through an encounter with the transformative forces of the spiritual world, and this is provided by the realm of the Tower of transformation.

Thus the alchemical wedding begun in the Castle can only be resolved and completed through the visit to, and work in, the spiritual realm of the Tower.

Below the inscription "Prince Hermes..." beside the Lion (see the Fourth Day), the following string of symbols appears:

∞ ≫ːＸＸ⊃ＩＣ⅄ⱳ≻⸫

On the sixth day, while engaged in the process in the Tower, Rosenkreutz notes another inscription on the side of a copper vessel, the concluding line of which is similar to the above, and which seems to be a coded date:

•өөө᷄4ⱦ⸝Ｘ❡≻.Ѳ╫・Ⅲb・Ⅲᴼ.ᵴⱦᵴ

Keinast suggested that this first inscription could be analysed as follows:

∞	= L =	50			⅄	= V =	5
>	= C =	100			ⱳ	= III =	3
ɔː	= C =	100			>	= C =	100
XX	= XX =	20					
ɔIC	= M =	1000			TOTAL	=	1378

giving 1378, the date of Christian Rosenkeutz's birth as given in the *Confessio*.

The second chronogram he analyses as follows:

~~1000~~	=	+	1000
<	=	−	100
I	=	−	1
L	=	+	50
X	=	+	10
O	=	+	500
TOTAL	=		1459

The Play within the Play

The play or comedy performed at the center of the allegory illustrates the main theme of the *Chemical Wedding*—that is, the need for humanity to rescue and make relationship with the feminine component of the soul which has to a great extent been repressed and lost. This play has seven acts with interludes between.

The old King finds a chest which contains the daughter of the royal family of a country adjacent to his own. This country has been overrun and usurped by the Moor. The old King brings up the young child.

Interlude: a Lion and Griffin fight, and the lion wins.

The Moor discovers this old King has the Princess under his charge. He mounts an expedition and gets her back into his power.

Interlude: Triumph or procession of the Moor.

An ancient Knight leads the King's party against the Moor and again rescues the young Princess. The old King declares that he has protected her, brought her up well (though she does not altogether behave herself), and wishes his son to marry her.

Interlude: Four Beasts of Daniel.

The young Princess is restored to her lost kingdom. She flirts with the ambassadors and courtiers, and is an easy prey to the Moor who ingratiates himself with her. Thus through her weakness he takes command again over her realm.

Interlude: Nebuchadnezzar's Image.

The young Prince, hearing what has befallen his spouse, calls for action. His father only sends ambassadors to intercede, whom she refuses to receive, admitting that she is the concubine of the Moor.

Interlude: Band of fools make up a Globe of the World.

The young Prince resolves to do battle with the Moor, yet not without danger to himself. For after the battle he appears to be dead; however, at length he is revived. He rescues his spouse and puts her in charge of his steward and chaplain, who treat her so badly he has to intervene.

Interlude: Elephant and Tower of Musicians.

The Bridegroom appears in great pomp and ceremony and is wedded to his Bride.

Thus we have in the first act the initial appearance of the feminine as a child princess deprived of her kingdom by a Moor. She is rescued and protected by the old male aspect of the soul, the ancient King. She is, however, recaptured by the black Moor who wishes to deprive her of her rights. But in act three, an ancient Knight from the King's realm re-rescues her. Now that she has grown up a little, we see that she is beginning to rebel against this patriarchal, though kindly, regime of old men and will not entirely conform to the old King's rules. The fourth act finds her reestablished in her kingdom, but now she wants to have a relationship as an equal with the masculine, and not be patronized by the support of the old King and his ancient Knight. In the absence of the Prince she turns to the Moor, who is willing to indulge her flirtations to get control over her again. Thus, in opposition to the old King's paternalism, she is taken advantage of by the Moor aspect of the masculine, characterized by its brutality and grasping for power. The old King sends his ambassadors to intercede, but she now recognizes that her faults have brought her into this terrible situation, and she will not see the ambassadors. Only the active intervention of the young Prince in rejecting his father's advice (the ambassadors) and challenging the Moor to battle can break through and make a true relationship with her. However, the Prince has to suffer a death and resurrection through his fight with the Moor. He next has to defend his Princess against the patriarchal bullying of the steward and chaplain, representatives of the old King's forces. Having worked through all these inner struggles, the masculine and feminine can make a new and equal relationship as Bride and Groom.

Thus the scheme of this little play sets the structure that underlies the form of the whole allegory. The interludes reflect in symbolic form the happenings in the play.

Venus, the Sirens' Song, and the Theme of Love

On the morning of the Fifth Day, Christian Rosenkreutz uncovers the sleeping body of Lady Venus, the Goddess of Love, hidden and sealed up in a mausoleum underneath the Castle. Later that day, when the company travel in a fleet of seven ships across the great lake, a host of sirens, nymphs and sea-goddesses come to them and begin to sing. In their song, which they direct particularly to the King whose body lies on board, they remind us that "here below" in the realm of the world there is nothing better than Love. It is the power of Love that makes us like to God. It is the power of Love that gives us life, that can transform two into one. They sing that only through the flame of Love can the soul and body of the King and Queen be re-conjoined.

Rosenkreutz is profoundly affected by this song and begins to swoon with giddiness. This he ascribes to the effects of Cupid and to the wound he received on his head during the dream on the evening of the First Day.

Thus we note that Christian Rosenkreutz is in a sense wounded three times in the allegory: first, on the head in his dream; next, on the hand by Cupid's dart; and third, inwardly in the heart by the Sirens' Song.

The author focuses on the theme of Love both immediately before and after the wedding-execution. Thus the trick played by the maidens upon the men, suggesting that if they might partner and sleep with each of them that night, then they would make them much the pleasanter in the morning, is a reference to the outer meeting of the polarities in sexuality, which is further suggested by the playful sport of Cupid on the Fourth Day. Christian Rosenkreutz's sight of Venus unveiled brings to him both a sense of outer physical beauty and also the indwelling power that lies in the force of Love. The Sirens further emphasize this element to him. Their song dwells upon this transformative power that lies in Love, and this they address particularly to the King. For it is through the King's denial of outer expression to the Love-forces bound up in the relationship of male and female, that he has to go through this ritual wedding-execution. Only when he has made a balanced relationship to the feminine through the power of Love can he be released from his awful destiny.

The Ascent of the Tower

The work undertaken in the Tower is obviously crucial to the whole process of transformation and resurrection. It involves an ascent of seven levels where the company of adepts participate in and experience the great work of spiritual transformation through seven stages. In this sense, the rise to another level of the Tower corresponds to their developing a more lofty spiritual insight. They are only able to ascend from one level to the next by using one of three instruments—wings, ladders, and ropes—which correspond to three different paths of spiritual development.

The adepts with 'wings' are those who can project their consciousness onto the spiritual level. This corresponds to the path of the mystic whose consciousness rises easily and naturally to the spiritual as if borne on wings. Those with 'ladders,' among whom we count Christian Rosenkreutz, strive rather to build a link in their souls between outer perception and an awareness of the spirit. This is a more Hermetic path. The adepts in the company using 'ropes' have a more outward-directed consciousness and must have some assistance from above, using the full force of their will to pull themselves against the gravity of a consciousness turned more to the outer world of perceptions. We can tentatively describe these as working more through the magical faculties, using the objects of outer ritual together with their strength of will to make the ascent.

Interestingly, on the first level of the Tower, the Warder seems initially to offer them a choice of these means of developing their consciousness, but decides instead to distribute them by the drawing of lots. Thus the choice of path for the adepts is not one that they can consciously make, but must leave in the hands of destiny or fate.

The first level is undertaken in the laboratory at the basement of the Tower, where Christian Rosenkreutz and his companions are set to preparing essences of stones and plants. However, the text hints at the fact that the true work of the first level was the death of the Kings and Queens, by indicating that simultaneously with their work at this level the bodies were being prepared by the maidens elsewhere in the Tower. The materials that the aspiring alchemists prepare are not the prima materia of the process, but substances containing the etheric essence of the life force which will later be brought on the seventh level to enliven the dead ashes of the prima materia.

The second level begins with a ritual procession around a great vessel which holds the royal bodies. Here we see arrayed in a pattern the 62 people involved: 40 maidens, 12 musicians, 9 alchemists, and the Virgin. For the completion of the whole process we have to add the Warder and Cupid, making 64 persons in all. The Virgin places the head of the Moor into the uppermost vessel, and the distillation of the essence of the bodies is begun. The maidens assist this with the heat of their lamps. This red essence is gathered into a large globe-like vessel and taken up to the third level.

Here it is heated by sunlight reflected in mirrors until eventually, once it has been thoroughly cooked, they open the globe and take out the substance of their work which has now formed itself into a great white egg.

On the fourth level this egg is placed in a square copper vessel.* (Copper is the metal of Venus, which also composed the triangular fountain vessel in the Sepulcher of Venus, seen on the Fifth Day.)

This egg hatches into a Bird which is initially naked but goes through three transformations of plumage by ingesting the blood of

---

* This vessel bears a strange inscription which has puzzled many commentators. Alfons Rosenberg in his modern German version of the text suggests the following:

OBLI(gatio). TO(lle). BIT(umen). MI(nutem). LI(quefactumque K or C(antione). I(gnique). VOLT(us). BIT(uminis). TO(llitur). GOLT.

Which would translate into "Prescription: Take pulverised and liquefied fusible bitumen; through music and fire the form of the bitumen is elevated to Gold." Although this is rather a speculative interpretation, it would seem at least to make sense of the inscription.

Montgomery suggests that the next fragmentary line "Sanitas Nix Hasta" is in fact a reference to Virgil's *Aeneid* (XII, line 396) "nixus in hastam." During this closing scene of the tale, Iapyx the healer appears and heals Aeneas, who has been wounded, with a medicine miraculously provided by Venus. Rosenberg expands the following line to

F(orma). I(gne). A(rteque). T(ransformatur)

"The form is transmuted through fire and the (alchemical) art." Although I do not believe that these interpretations add anything substantial to our understanding of the work, I include them for the sake of completeness.

the Royal victims, which as we recall was at the execution collected separately in golden cups. These three feedings of the Bird with the blood from the three Royal couples produce in sequence a black stage, then a white, then multi-colored feathers. These are the well-known alchemical stages of the Nigredo (sometimes known as the Black Crow), the Albedo (also known as the White Swan), and the multi-colored phase of the Peacock's Tail.

On level five this Bird is placed in a bath colored with a white powder so as to appear as milk. The bath is heated and the feathers of the Bird dissolve and tinge the liquid blue. They take the Bird, now smooth and featherless from the bath, and boil away the liquid till it forms a blue stone, with which they proceed to paint their Bird all over, except for the head which they leave white.

Thus on the fourth level the Bird, through ingesting the blood of the Royal couples, outwardly manifested this as a cycle of color changes in its plumage. Now on the fifth level, this outer plumage is removed in the bath and formed into a blue stone, and with this they are able to paint the Bird a blue color that it was not able to create out of itself.

On the sixth level, the Bird is taken before the altar and its ritual objects. There it drinks of the fountain, and pecks at the serpent in the skull. This allows the operators to gather the serpent's blood and feed it to the Bird, even though it is reluctant to drink it. They wait for the ritual moment when the clock will strike the third conjunction marked by the turning globe, then the Bird lies down voluntarily upon the Book and suffers its head to be cut off. Its blood is collected in a golden cup, while its body is burnt to ashes by a flame kindled at the ever-burning taper. This event on the sixth floor is a kind of recapitulation on a higher level of the beheading on the Fourth Day, and the link is further established through the involvement, as before, of the altar and its objects in the ritual.

Here a break occurs, with Christian Rosenkreutz and three others being tricked into thinking that they have failed in the work; however, it is rather the other alchemists who are deceived into believing that they will experience the summit of the Magnum Opus whereas they merely attain the work of transmuting metals. Rosenkreutz and the other specially chosen three are taken by some winding stairs to the true seventh level, where they are given the task of resurrecting the King and Queen under the guidance of the Warder of the Tower, who enters the process for the first time. They begin with the ashes of the dead Bird which they moisten with the essences of plants and stones prepared in the laboratory of the first level, to form a dough which they heat over a fire and cast into two little molds and leave to cool. When they open these forms, they find inside two perfectly formed little images of a man and a woman, the appearance of which Rosenkreutz compares with the flesh of Lady Venus. These they nourish with the blood of the Bird, and these shapes began to increase quickly both in size and in fairness of form, until soon they come to surpass even the beauty of Venus. However, they remain non-living forms until, after many ceremonies, a stream of fire is directed into them from the topmost dome of the Tower. Three times each figure is enlivened by this descent of the living flames from the top of the Tower, and once this is completed, they are taken out and placed in a bed. Cupid, who till now has not been seen in the Tower, appears and awakens them from their sleep, and the Virgin clothes them in strange garments that seem to be made of crystal.

The work of resurrection is thus completed.

This Tower is named Olympus, the classical abode of the gods and goddesses who live eternally on the divine ambrosia. So we can picture this as the spiritual world, the world of the gods. The events outlined in this sequence of symbols are actually taking place on the spiritual level. The events in the Castle on the other hand should be seen as happening within the astral world of the human soul, while the world from which Rosenkreutz comes initially is the world of outer perceptions.

The 'death' process in the soul pictured by the beheading of the Bride and Groom can only be healed through a process taking place in the spiritual realm, that is in the Tower of Olympus. The symbolic description makes understanding this from the outside very difficult, and readers will have to work inwardly with this symbolic process of the ascent of the Tower if they are to truly grasp its essence. I can only give here a few suggestions as to ways we can approach this cycle from the outside.

Again, while planetary correspondences to these seven levels might seem appropriate, the reader will find this unproductive of new insights. The process seems rather to mirror the archetypal sevenfold process I outlined earlier.

The initial stage is the death of the King and Queen. Now a physical death is actually a birth in the spiritual world, for when a being is released from its material envelope it returns to a more spiritual state. The corpses of the Kings and Queens are brought together on level two and their polarities are resolved by being distilled into a single substance. This is the true alchemical wedding, where these two facets are married in the most complete way possible through a mutual dissolution. This, on being cooked by the heat of the Sun, gives rise to a new synthesis, the Egg, and at the fourth stage this hatches out new life in the form of the Bird. The Bird, the new manifestation of the King and Queen forces, is nourished at this point with the blood, the living spiritual essence of the King and Queen, and undergoes transformation as it, in turn, reflects the essence of these archetypes in its plumage. In the next stage, the Bird experiences an opposition or check to the manifestation of its own being (not being allowed to develop its ability to fly), and is boiled in a vessel, thus losing its lovely plumage. Thus it is chained and not allowed freedom to fly, and the agents through which it could fly, its feathers, are boiled down and reduced to a blue stone. On the sixth level the Bird is sacrificed, and two things result from this: its essential blood, and the ashes of its body.

So we see here that from the bodies of the King and Queen a composite substance was created which when formed into an egg then gave birth to the Bird. This Bird is thus a new spiritual embodiment of the King and Queen, the reflection of their bodies in the spiritual world. Had this Bird been allowed to develop freely, then it would have had its own independent life in the spiritual world. The alchemists must now force it back into incarnation, by first removing its feathers so that it cannot soar into the higher spiritual realms; later, on the sixth level of the Tower, by sacrificing it and extracting a twofold essence in its ashes and blood. Thus the

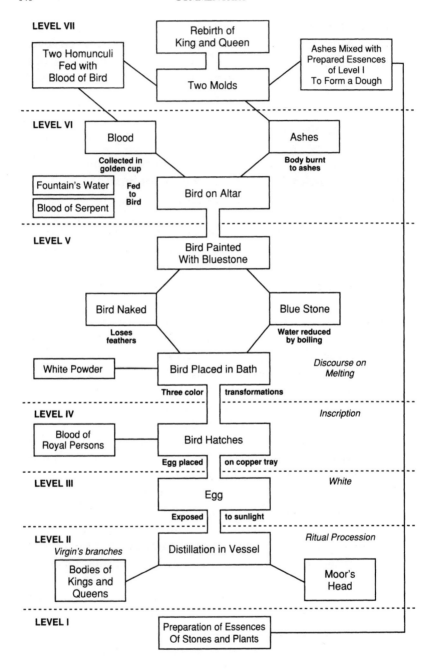

LEVEL VII

Two Homunculi Fed with Blood of Bird

Rebirth of King and Queen

Two Molds

Ashes Mixed with Prepared Essences of Level I To Form a Dough

LEVEL VI

Blood

Collected in golden cup

Ashes

Body burnt to ashes

Fountain's Water

Blood of Serpent

Fed to Bird

Bird on Altar

LEVEL V

Bird Painted With Bluestone

Bird Naked

Loses feathers

Blue Stone

Water reduced by boiling

White Powder

Bird Placed in Bath

Discourse on Melting

Three color

transformations

LEVEL IV

Inscription

Blood of Royal Persons

Bird Hatches

Egg placed

on copper tray

LEVEL III

White

Egg

Exposed

to sunlight

LEVEL II

Ritual Procession

Virgin's branches

Distillation in Vessel

Bodies of Kings and Queens

Moor's Head

LEVEL I

Preparation of Essences Of Stones and Plants

upward spiritual ascent of the metamorphosed forces of the King and Queen into higher and higher regions of the spirit is halted and they are brought back into incarnation, having risen to a certain stage of spiritualization in this Bird form that has transcended the state of duality they experienced in the Castle.

On the upward arc we have no new substances brought into the work. All evolves out of the conjoined bodies of the Kings and Queens. On the downward arc into new incarnation, we find however three ingestions of blood—the Blood of the Royal Persons, the Blood of the Serpent, and the Blood of the Bird. In alchemical terms, this blood is the highest development of substance on the earthly realm. To alchemists, the blood of any being is its highest material vehicle. Blood is the closest form that substance can attain to a spiritual state. So by feeding the process, on the arc of its descent into matter, with these three types of blood, the operators are bringing to the process the highest and most subtle substance as a vehicle into which the spiritual essence of the King and Queen can reincarnate. This spiritual essence or blood was in fact separated from their bodies earlier in the process, so in a sense this is merely a reconnection with that which they lost during the death process.

Working further with the Chemical Wedding

The picture I have outlined above may seem a rather abstract and remote process, possessing few points of contact with our consciousness today; however, this is not so. If we wish to work further with the process and perform the alchemical wedding in our own being, this can still be done.

It means that we, like Christian Rosenkreutz, must find the King and Queen within ourselves. This King is the expression of an unintegrated masculine archetype, who is frightened of the elemental power of the feminine and resorts to an outward and insecure patriarchy in order to distance himself from the primal forces he fears might engulf and devour him. The Queen is the expression of an unintegrated feminine archetype, who is so unsure of her powers that she bows down and accepts the patriarchal values of the King's domain. In a sense she has lost her own kingdom (like the Princess in the play), but instead has some shadow of power in the realm of the King. Now these two aspects work in all of us, and if we are in any way spiritually honest with ourselves, and have enough humility to allow our introspection to penetrate deeply into our souls, we will all be able to recognize these figures and the various ways in which they manifest in our personalities.

Having recognized the King and Queen in our souls, and having, like Christian Rosenkreutz, entered the realm of our inner soul Castle, then we can begin the alchemical wedding if we have the will.

This requires an initial beheading. We have to cut off the power of these archetypes, by recognizing their imbalance and knowing that they must die in order that our souls can live and attain more harmonious energies. Of course, this is not something that can be achieved at one stroke of an inner Moor's axe, but is, rather, a continual process we have to be prepared to undertake upon ourselves. It will require our keenness of will.

We have to try to inwardly fuse the King and Queen facets together, by initially merging together the lower aspect of their energies, their corpses or bodies. Their essences, their blood, however, remain separate at this initial stage. In our meditation, by opening ourselves and seeking new experiences, we try to recognize the ways in which the King and Queen facets of our inner life can lose their unbalanced power and dissolve together. Once we have some sense of this dissolving together of our inner forces, then we must look for a new synthesis forming itself. This is pictured in the *Chemical Wedding* as the Egg, but this experience could clothe itself in many other symbols reflecting our individual spiritual path and inner landscape. By exposing our dissolved King and Queen to the inner fire of our meditation, the egg is formed which gives birth to the Bird.

This Bird is a certain power within our souls that has the ability to soar upwards into the spiritual world. Many people who have achieved the 'Bird' stage, perhaps through other inner journeys not so consciously undertaken, find that they often seem to be carried out of themselves and suddenly presented with some fleeting spiritual experience. Such fleeting spiritual experiences can be disturbing as well as enlightening, but often this Bird is quite out of control within us. It suddenly swoops within our souls and we have to go with the experience. All of us must have at some time met people who symbolically have this uncontrolled Bird within them, and often we wish that they could keep it under some restraint! Some people do get stuck on this level and end up tripping out into fascinating symbolic wonderlands, entirely remote from our real world! The next stage of the process of the alchemical wedding is to 'earth' the bird in our souls and not allow it to soar into elevated and remote spiritual heights. The great occultists and mystics are those who have been able to experience symbolically this bird in their souls, using it, but not becoming identified with it or becoming the puppet of its erratic flightiness. Of course, these occultists and mystics often used other symbols and inner pictures to describe this stage—the symbol of the Bird is itself inessential and merely one way of portraying this subtle inner experience.

Like the operators in the Tower, we have to sacrifice the Bird within ourselves if we are to carry forward this spiritualization process into incarnation. For this Bird lives in the highest astral realms of our souls which border upon the spiritual world. The Bird thus links the spiritual world with our higher astral realm. If we are to progress further and be able to bring spiritual insights into outer manifestation we have to bring this down into our lower vehicles. This is the task of the last level in the Tower. The ashes of the Bird, its lowest embodiment (the lowest astral realm), are separated from its blood (the spiritual essence that would drive it higher), and these ashes are mixed with the highest essences of the plant and mineral kingdom. What is represented here are the forces of our etheric bodies, for at this point we have to bring the Bird experience into our etheric bodies through certain meditative exercises. These will arise naturally through a rhythmic working with the process, but the effectiveness can be increased by certain special meditations that work directly into the etheric body. However this is achieved, in time and with perseverance, the essence of the Bird can be woven into our etheric bodies, forming there a pattern which will eventually become quite solid and firm. Then, instead of having to trust the flightiness of the Bird experience, we will possess a pattern in our etheric bodies which reflects the spiritual world that we can touch upon quite consciously. This is the Golden Stone, the Stone of the Alchemical Philosophers, which arises in our being only through the process of involution, of incarnating the spiritual in our lower vehicles. Thus the inner flow of polarities within our souls becomes tinged and transformed. No longer are we the victims of the power of these polarities, always falling into dualistic projections, but instead we have a conscious sense of the spiritual power of these polarities. This, of course, is pictured in the rebirth of the King and Queen within us: not the return of the old distorted unbalanced polarities, but instead a newly born King and Queen who have met each other inwardly, and through having dissolved mutually into one another, have known each other in the most intimate way. (There is a parallel with this in the *Rosarium Philosophorum* process.) This reborn King and Queen within our souls are manifestations of the one unity, being inwardly linked in the higher regions of our souls; and now, even in their lowest manifestation, they have a balance and respect for each other's forces.

This is a picture of the great task of inner development outlined in the *Chemical Wedding*.

The Links of the Chemical Wedding *with Goethe's* Fairy Tale of the Green Snake and the Beautiful Lily

In a letter written in 1786 to Charlotte von Stein, Goethe mentioned that he saw in the *Chemical Wedding* the makings of a good story:

> There will be a good fairy-tale to tell at the right time, but it will have to be reborn, it can't be enjoyed in its old skin.

The parallels are, however, not very obvious, certainly as regards their form, though both are allegories of inner transformation and work with the same material. The links hinge rather on the common theme of the relationship of the male and female facets of our inner nature. The male part feels threatened and endangered even to its death by the primal energies of the feminine. Thus in both allegories, the male figure of the King or young Prince has to undergo a death through too close an encounter with the feminine, and has to be resurrected by a concerted ritual activity of the other characters. This provides the dramatic focus of both works. In the *Chemical Wedding*, the corpses have to travel across a great lake to the Tower of Olympus in order to carry out the resurrection, while in Goethe's *Fairy Tale* the company have to cross the Great River and enter the underground Temple. The ascent of the Tower of Olympus in this sense corresponds to the sequence of the raising of the underground Temple and its establishment firmly on the other bank of the River. There are other parallels which the reader may find interesting to pursue. (See my *Commentary on Goethe's Fairy Tale*, Magnum Opus Hermetic Sourceworks, No. 14.)

Goethe alters the theme of the *Chemical Wedding* significantly, making it reflect his own political and social views. Therefore, in his *Fairy Tale* a permanent change seems to have been brought about through the refounding of the Temple and the building of the bridge connecting the two realms. The interaction and resolution on a high archetypal level brings about a permanent change in the human soul. The *Chemical Wedding* treats the matter differently, leaving the situation at the close much the same as it was at the beginning, and we have the distinct impression that the inhabitants of the Castle have to continue going through the cycle endlessly. Thus the *Chemical Wedding* wants to make us aware of the need for us to continually work the process of inner transformation; Goethe has a different, perhaps more romantic and modern view, that these inner changes can be achieved once and for all, almost like a revolutionary social change or an irreversible modification in our environment. The view of the Rosicrucian philosophy behind the *Chemical Wedding* seems rather that the human soul has to work eternally through this inner rebirth. As it stresses this need for us to develop individually by identifying with Christian Rosenkreutz on his inner journey, it is perhaps the more valuable as a source for the practical work of soul transformation.

The Links with the Parabola *of Hinricus Madathanus*

The *Parabola* of the Rosicrucian writer Hinricus Madathanus (=Adrian von Mynsicht, c. 1590–1638), first published in 1625, uses the same archetypal process of transformation as is outlined in the *Chemical Wedding*, though it does not use precisely the same outward description. It is not a paraphrased or reworked version of the *Chemical Wedding*, but an independently conceived allegory using this same underlying archetypal transformation process. Careful study of the parallels may help to cast some further light upon the Rosicrucian spiritual transformation process that both these authors contrived to put before us, wrapped up and clothed in their different symbols. I cannot comment here on the *Parabola* in depth but will merely point the reader to the more obvious parallels. The complete text of the *Parabola* is included as an appendix.

Parabola	*Chemical Wedding*
Wind blows hero along a narrow footpath	Christian Rosenkreutz is forced along one of the four ways
Meeting with the old men	The guests in the Hall
Roses in hat	Roses in hat
Enters garden and meets maiden and youth	Audience with King and Queen
Wedding bed is a prison in which youth and maiden die	Beheading at the wedding
Hero sets about resurrecting the youth and maiden (reference here to Medea and Jason, the seeker of the Golden Fleece)	Process in the tower undertaken by the Knights of the Golden Fleece
Different colored robes	Color changes during the process in the tower (bird's plumage)
Reference to the benefitting of fellow men through the results of the process	Precepts of the Order of the Golden Stone

Conclusion

I hope that the commentary I have presented here may at least provide some suggestions as to ways in which we can approach the inner content of this elaborate allegory. I have not intended to pull the structure to pieces and examine each symbol on its own, but wished rather to look at the symbolic events in the context they appear within the allegory. As I indicated at the beginning of this commentary, I do not believe that this greatest of all Hermetic allegories can be reduced to mere intellectual architecture; indeed, it is my contention that the allegory must be reborn within our souls, by living with it in our imaginations, if we are to truly gain anything from this work. This commentary has been written out of such an immersion in the symbols, and should provide some pointers for others to undertake similar explorations. The view I present here is in no sense the only one, and other inner explorers will journey through the allegory in their own ways, reflecting their own abilities and individual creative spirits. This ability of the *Chemical Wedding* to support many different interpretations is an indication of the spiritual strength and integrity of the allegory.

I have not attempted to enter into the question of chronology. On the title page the date 1459 is given for the events of this tale. Integrating this with the chronology of the *Fama* (in which Christian Rosenkreutz is shown to have been born in 1378 and to have died in 1484 at the grand old age of 106), we see that Christian Rosenkreutz achieved this initiation when he was 81. We remember that after he died in 1484 he remained buried in his tomb for 120 years until, in 1604, this was uncovered and the Rosicrucian wisdom was revealed. It is thought that the *Chemical Wedding* was originally sketched in outline around about 1604. I believe we should come to see all this chronology as symbolic, indicating rhythmic cycles in time during which the esoteric Hermetic wisdom at the heart of Rosicrucianism alternatively lay hidden in a phase of inward withdrawal (in the tomb of C.R.) and then appeared as an overt cultural current in the outer world.

The 120 years during which Christian Rosenkreutz lay in his tomb corresponds to the cycle of 120 years which Simon Studion (the millenialist author of an elaborate system of occult numerology bearing upon Rosicrucianism) indicated in his *Naometria* manuscript as being the basis for the unfolding of spiritual impulses in time. Studion also identified the year 1604 as central to his thesis and undoubtedly his work provides the basis for Rosicrucian chronology. It will be found to be an interesting exercise to follow up these cycles and map them through into our present age.

When we contemplate this allegory we will find many puzzles and enigmas; however, perhaps the most perplexing among these is the place of Christianity in this 'Rosicrucianism' of the tale. Our initial thought that this allegory has woven into it the threads of an 'esoteric Christianity' is not so easy to follow through the edifice of symbolism, and it is difficult indeed to find any conventional Christian message. The events unfold like an ancient Greek or Egyptian initiation ritual rather than incorporating definitive Christian elements, such as atonement and redemption through the suffering of a Christ figure for the sins of the world. For example, it will not do to identify the young King as a Christ archetype, for there seems little sense of his suffering, but merely his awareness that he has to undergo a ritual death and rebirth, and in no sense does he take upon himself the burden of the sins of others. It seems that we have to look deeper for the Christian content, as it does not lie on the surface of the symbolism.

I believe we can find a way to approach this through the role of the feminine in the *Chemical Wedding*. As I have shown throughout my commentary, the balancing of the feminine and masculine in the human soul lies at the heart of the process of inner transformation outlined in the *Chemical Wedding*. The exoteric Christianity of the Church had by the Middle Ages rigidified into a patriarchal structure controlled by a masculine priesthood. Despite the impulse of Grail Christianity in the 12th–13th centuries, which showed the need for Christian humanity to experience and balance their masculine and feminine sides, the outer Church had deepened its patriarchal structure until, in the early 16th century, it so repressed freedom of thought that the Protestant movement was born and a new impulse was given to Christianity through Luther. Although this new movement initially seemed to promise a new freedom for the human spirit, sadly this was not to be, for its leaders proved to be even more rigid and patriarchal than those of Rome, and created instead merely another dualistic religion to enslave the human soul.

The essence of Christianity, which I believe lies in inner transformation, was not to be found in this new Protestantism, but merely the outer trappings of a dualistic religion, in which there was even less spiritual space for experiencing that balance of the masculine and feminine which lay at the center of the transmutation of the soul. Rosicrucianism seems to have arisen as an antithesis to the development of the codified Protestantism of Luther and Calvin. This outer Christianity focused on the Cross of Suffering of Christ, and impressed upon Western humanity an eternal sense of failing to live up to impossible ideals of conduct, the shame of 'sin.' As human beings we were impressed to feel a deep shame that Christ, the Son of God, had been made to suffer and die for our 'sins,' and was still suffering through each 'sin' we committed. The whole focus of this Protestant religion was on the darkness of this suffering—Christ on the Cross. Rosicrucianism tried to establish a new symbol in the soul of humanity—to set the Rose upon the Cross. Instead of meditating upon the bleeding, mangled, suffering body of Christ crucified, Rosicrucianism called upon us to set a living Rose, as a symbol of resurrection and transformation, upon the Cross. This Rose is also a symbol of the feminine placed on the masculine cross. It has links with the Rose Garden of the Virgin in Catholicism; the domain of the feminine Sophia; and the *Rosarium Philosophorum*, the Rosary of the Alchemical Philosophers, in which the interweaving of the masculine and feminine into the Hermetic androgyne was central to the inner transmutation of Alchemy. The Rosicrucian symbol of the Rose on the Cross thus points to an esotericism which involves an inner encounter with the masculine and feminine components of our inner nature, and the active integration of these, which leads to our inner growth and spiritual development. The Rosicrucians sought to integrate the cold masculine forces of the head, the intellect, with all its dangers of remoteness and icy, external, formal thought, with the hot passionate energies of our earthy soul nature (often pictured as feminine), the unpredictable, ever-flowing emotional currents that are the vital energies of our life forces.

The printer's colophon of the *Chemical Wedding* provides, I believe, a symbolic statement of the way in which the Rosicrucians sought to resolve this seeming paradox of the battle of the masculine and feminine in our souls. Here we see an inverted anchor, upon which sits a bird. In Rosicrucian terms we must anchor our thinking in the spiritual world, and not let our thought merely drift in the remote intellectualism of form unconnected with spirit. The bird is that facet in the heights of our souls that can rise and mediate with the highest realms of the spirit.

Around the shaft of the anchor is entwined a snake representing the more feminine forces within our being. These 'lower' or rather 'primal' earthy energies of our psyches must, in Rosicrucian esoteric practice, be effectively earthed and not merely allowed to eternally flow and ebb wheresoever they will. Thus the head of the snake rests upon the solid foundation of the Stone, the Stone of the Philosophers which provides the inner ground for the forces of the Soul to rest and measure themselves upon.

Those who possess this inner stone are no longer the victims of their ever-flowing soul forces, but have a still center in their being around which to build lasting spiritual forms out of their volatile primal energies—the inner mercury of the soul. In this sense, Rosicrucianism is that esoteric philosophy lying at the heart of Western Hermeticism which provides a path for the balancing and integration of the masculine and feminine aspects of our souls, and the inner meeting of the lofty intellect with the primal earthy energies at the center of our being.

There would seem to be a definite link with the work of Heinrich Khunrath, for he employed in his early book entitled *Chaos* (1597) the same Latin phrase as is found on the title page of the first editions of the *Chemical Wedding*, "Mysteries made public become cheap." Much of the symbolic material of the *Chemical Wedding* was prefigured in engravings to Heinrich Khunrath's *Amphitheatre of Eternal Wisdom*. These nine engravings published during the period 1602–1609 parallel to a great extent the events in the *Chemical Wedding*. (See the *Amphitheatre Engravings of Heinrich Kunrath*, Magnum Opus Hermetic Series, No. 7.) The first plate shows the initiate seeking his way to the College of the Mysteries. On his way, he converses with a company of fellow travellers before a pyramidal slab of stone bearing the verses of the *Emerald Tablet* of Hermes Trismegistus. Next, he enters the Gate of the Mysteries, ascending seven steps (echoing perhaps the weighing ceremony). Another plate shows the initiate being besieged by calumniators who press against him all sorts of libels. This reminds us of the scene in the Hall of guests. The next plate is that of the Heptangular Fortress of Alchemy which has three gates or portals like the Castle of the *Chemical Wedding*. Above the last of these gates is seen the Hieroglyphic Monad ☿, the sign shown to Christian Rosenkreutz upon his invitation to the Wedding. The next plate shows us a scene such as we can imagine the interior of the Castle to be, with an oratory for prayer and a furnace for the alchemical work; on a central table are musical instruments, also important in the Castle of the Bridegroom. The following plate could be seen to parallel the process in the Tower of Olympus, as a hermaphrodite is shown being born out of a great egg, and a bird also is seen arising out of the process. The plate after this shows an integration of various facets of the work into one unity, while the final engraving depicts the symbol of Christ within the Cosmic Rose. This is not a symbol of a crucified suffering Christ, but that of the resurrected reborn Christ.

It is this profoundly positive view of the powers latent in the human soul that we come to see as lying at the heart of Rosicrucianism. The *Chemical Wedding* reminds us of the potential in our souls for this inner transformation, resurrection, and spiritual rebirth.

This power of our inner transmutation, our resurrection and rebirth to the spirit, lies within each of our souls if only we go on our inner quest and participate in the *Chemical Wedding*, to which all of us are eternally invited.

The Parabola is an anonymous translation from *The Secret Symbols of the Rosicrucians*.

Appendix

The Parabola of Hinricus Madathanus Theosophus

As I once was walking in a beautiful, green, young forest, meditating and deploring the difficulties of this life, considering how, through the grievous Fall of our first Parents we came into such wretchedness and grief, I left the accustomed road and came, I know not how, upon a narrow footpath, very rough, untrodden, difficult and overgrown with so many bushes and brambles that it was easy to see it was very seldom used. At this I became frightened and wished to retrace my steps. But this was not possible, especially since a strong wind blew so mightily behind me that I had to take ten steps forward for every one I could take backward. Therefore I had to press on, despite the roughness of the way.

After advancing thus for a good while, I came at last to a lovely meadow, encircled by beautiful fruit-laden trees, and called by the inhabitants, The Field of the Blessed. Here I met a group of old men with snow-white beards, and one among them was young and had a pointed black beard. A still younger man was present also, whose name I knew, but whose face I did not yet see. These men conversed about many things, particularly about a high and great secret in Nature which God kept hidden from the multitude, revealing it only to the few who loved Him. I listened to them for a long time, and their words pleased me much. But some among them appeared to mutter foolishly, indeed not about the objectives or the work, but about Parabolas, Similitudes and other Parergons. In this they followed the Figmenta of Aristotle, of Pliny and of others, each of whom had copied from the other. At this I could no longer remain silent, but put in a word of my own, answering many futile things on the basis of experience, so that many listened to me, examining me in their speciality, putting me to some very hard tests. But my foundation was so good that I came through with all honors, whereat they all were amazed. However they unanimously accepted me into their Brotherhood, whereat I rejoiced heartily.

But they said that I could not be a full colleague so long as I did not know their Lion and was not fully aware of what he could do internally and externally. I was therefore to set about diligently to make him submissive to myself. Confidently I promised them I would do my best, for I enjoyed their company so much that I would not have parted from them for anything in the world.

So they led me to the Lion and very carefully described him to me. But what I was to do with him at first, no one would tell me. Indeed some of them did give me certain hints, but so confusedly that not one in a thousand could understand them. However, when I had tied him and made certain that his sharp claws and pointed teeth could not harm me, they no longer kept anything back. The Lion was very old, fierce and huge; his yellow mane hung over his neck, and he really appeared unconquerable. I was nearly terror-stricken, and had it not been for my agreement and for the old men who stood around me to see how I would begin, I would have run away. Confidently I approached the lion in his cave and began to cajole him, but he looked at me so sharply with his glittering eyes that I nearly let my water for fear. At the same time I remembered that as we went to the Lion's cave one of the old men had told me that many people had attempted to conquer the Lion, but very few had succeeded. Since I did not wish to fail, I recalled many grips I had learned through careful application to athletics, and in addition I was well trained in natural magic, so I forgot about the pleasantries and attacked the Lion so artfully and subtly that before he was aware of it, I had pressed the blood out of his body, indeed out of his heart itself. The blood was beautifully red, but very choleric. But I examined his anatomy further and found many things which greatly surprised me; his bones were white as snow, and they were of greater quantity than his blood.

When my old men, standing round the cave and watching me, realized what I had done, they began to dispute with each other violently so that I could see their gestures. But what they said I could not understand because I was so far inside the cave. And when they began to shout at each other, I heard one who cried, "He must also bring the Lion to life again; otherwise he cannot be our colleague."

I did not wish to make trouble. Therefore I walked out of the cave and crossed a broad space. Then I came, I do not know how, to a very high wall which rose over a hundred ells into the clouds. But above there it did not have the width of a shoe. From the beginning where I started, to the end, there ran an iron railing along the top of the wall, well-fastened with many supports. I walked along the top of this wall and thought I saw someone going along a little ahead of me on the right side of the railing.

After I followed him a while, I saw someone following behind me on the other side of the railing (to this day I don't know whether it was a man or a woman) who called to me and said that it was better to walk on his side than where I was going. I easily believed this, for the railing which stood in the middle of the wall made the passageway very narrow so that it was difficult to walk along it at such a height. Then behind me I saw some people who wanted to go that same way. So I swung myself under the railing, holding it fast with both hands, and continued along the other side until I came to a place on the wall where it was especially dangerous to descend. Now I regretted that I had not remained on the other side; for I could not pass under the railing again; also it was impossible to turn back and take the other way again. Therefore I summoned my courage, trusted in my sure-footedness, held on tightly, and descended without harm. When I went on for a while, I had indeed forgotten about all dangers and also did not know where the wall and railing had vanished.

After I had descended I saw standing a lovely rosebush on which beautiful red and white roses were growing; but there were more of the red than of the white. I broke off some of them and put them on my hat.

I soon saw a wall encircling a great garden, in which were young fellows. Their maidens also would have liked to be in the garden, but they did not wish to make the great effort of walking the long distance around the wall to the gate. I was sorry for them and returned the whole distance I had come, then followed a smoother path, and I went so fast that I soon came to several houses, where I hoped to find the cottage of the gardener. There I found many people; each had his own room; often two were working together

slowly and diligently; but each had his own work. And it appeared
to me that all this they were doing, I had done before them, and that
I knew it all very well.

Then I thought, "Look, if so many other people do such dirty and
slovenly work only for appearance's sake, and each according to his
own ideas, but not established in Nature, then you yourself are
forgiven."

Therefore I would not stay there any longer for I knew that such
art would disappear in smoke, so I continued on my destined way.

As I now went toward the garden gate some looked at me sourly,
and I feared that they would hinder me in the fulfillment of my
intentions. Others, however, said, "See, he wishes to go into the
garden; but we who worked for so long in its service have never
entered it. We shall laugh at him if he blunders."

But I paid no attention to them, for I knew the plan of the garden
better than they, although I had never been in it, and I went straight
up to the gate. This was locked fast, and one could not discover even
a key-hole from the outside. But in the gate I saw a tiny round hole
which one could not distinguish with ordinary eyes, and I thought
it was necessary to open the gate there. I took out my skeleton-key,
especially prepared for this purpose, unlocked the gate and walked
in. After I was inside the gate I found more locked gates, but I
unlocked them without more difficulty. But I found that this was
a hallway as if it were in a well-built house, about six shoes wide
and twenty long, covered with a ceiling. And although the other
gates were still locked, I could see through them sufficiently into
the garden as soon as the first gate was opened.

And so in God's Name I wandered further into the garden. There
in the midst of it I found a little flower-bed, square, each of its four
sides six measuring-rods long, and covered with rosebushes, on
which the roses were blossoming beautifully. Since it had rained a
little and the sun was shining, a very lovely rainbow appeared. After
I left the flower-bed and had come to the place where I was to help
the maidens, behold! instead of the walls there stood a low wattled
fence. And the most beautiful maiden, dressed all in white satin,
with the most handsome youth, clad in scarlet, went past the rose-
garden, one leading the other by the arm and carrying many fragrant

roses in their hands. I spoke to them, asking how they had come over the fence.

"My dearest bridegroom here helped me over," she said, "and now we are leaving this lovely garden to go to our room to be together."

"I am happy," I replied, "that without further effort of mine you can satisfy your wish. Nevertheless you can see how I ran so long a way in so short a time, only to serve you."

After this I came into a great mill, built within stone walls; inside were no flour-bins nor any other things necessary for milling; moreover, through the wall one saw no water-wheels turning in the stream. I asked myself how this state of affairs came about, and one old miller answered me that the milling-machinery was locked up on the other side. Then I saw the miller's helper go into it by a covered passage-way, and I followed close after him. But as I was going along the passage, with the water-wheels on my left, I paused, amazed at what I saw there. For now the water-wheels were above the level of the passage, the water was coal-black, although the drops from it were white, and the covered passage-way itself was not more than three fingers wide. Nevertheless I risked turning back, holding fast to the beams over the passage-way; thus I crossed over the water safely. Then I asked the old miller how many water-wheels he had. He answered, Ten. This adventure I long remembered and dearly wished I could know what it meant. But when I saw that the miller would not reveal anything, I went on my way.

In front of the mill there arose a high, paved hill; on its summit some of the old men I have mentioned were walking in the warm sunshine. They had a letter from the Brotherhood and were discussing it among themselves. I soon guessed its contents, and that it might concern me, so I went to them and asked, "Sirs, does what you read there concern me?"

"Yes," they replied, "Your wife whom you recently married, you must keep in wedlock or we shall have to report it to the Prince."

I said, "That will be no trouble, for I was born together with her, as it were, was raised with her as a child, and because I have married her I shall keep her always, and death itself shall not part us. For I love her with all my heart."

"What have we to complain of, then?" they asked; "the bride is also happy, and we know her wish is that you must be joined together."

"I am very happy," I replied.

"Well then," said one of them, "the Lion will come back to life, mightier and more powerful than before."

Then I recalled my previous struggle and effort, and for some curious reason I felt this did not concern me but another whom I knew well. At that moment I saw our bridegroom walking with his bride, dressed as before, ready and prepared for the wedding, whereat I was very happy; for I had greatly feared that these things might concern me.

When, as has been said, our scarlet-clad bridegroom came to the old men with his dear bride, her white garments gleaming brightly, they were soon united and I greatly wondered that the maiden who might be the bridegroom's mother was nevertheless so young that she seemed newly born, as it were.

Now I do not know how the two had sinned; perhaps as brother and sister, united in love in such a way that they could not be separated, they had been accused of incest. Instead of a bridal bed and brilliant wedding they were condemned to a strong and ever-lasting prison. However, because of their noble birth and station, in order that they could do nothing together in secret, and so all their doings would always be visible to their guard, their prison was transparent-clear like crystal and round like a heavenly dome. But before they were placed inside, all the clothing and jewels they wore were taken from them so they had to live together stripped naked in their prison. No one was assigned to serve them, but all their necessities of food and drink—the latter drawn from the stream mentioned above—were placed inside before the door of the room was securely closed, locked, sealed with the seal of the Brotherhood, and I was placed on guard outside. And since winter was near I was to heat the room properly so they would neither freeze nor burn, but under no conditions could they come out of the room and escape. But if any harm resulted from my neglect of these instructions, I would undoubtedly receive great and severe punishment.

I did not feel well about this, my fear and worry made me faint-hearted, and I thought to myself, "It is no small task which has been assigned to me." I also knew that the Brotherhood did not lie, always did what it said, and certainly performed its work with diligence. However, I could change nothing, and besides, the locked room was situated in the midst of a strong tower, encircled by strong bulwarks and high walls, and since one could warm the room by a moderate but constant fire, I took up my task in God's Name, beginning to heat the room in order to protect the imprisoned married couple from the cold.

But what happened?—As soon as they felt the faintest breath of warmth, they embraced each other so lovingly that the like of it will not be seen again. And they remained together in such ardor that the heart of the young bridegroom disappeared in burning love, and his entire body melted and sank down in the arms of his beloved. When the latter, who had loved him no less than he had loved her, saw this, she began to lament, weeping bitterly over him and, so to say, buried him in such a flood of tears that one could no longer see what had happened to him. But her lamenting and weeping lasted only for a short time, for because of her great heart-sorrow she did not wish to live longer, and died of her own free will.

Ah, woe is me! In what anxiety, grief and distress was I when I saw those two I was to have helped, dissolved entirely to water and lying before me dead. Certain failure was there before my eyes, and moreover, what to me was the bitterest, and what I feared most were the coming taunts and sneers, as well as the punishment I would have to undergo.

I passed a few days in careful thought, considering what I could do, when I recalled how Medea had restored the corpse of Jason to life, and so I asked myself, "If Medea could do it, why cannot you do it also?"

Whereat I began to think how to proceed with it, but I did not find any better method than to maintain a steady warmth until the water would recede and I could see the dead bodies of the lovers once again. Then I hoped that I would escape all danger to my great gain and praise. Therefore for forty days I continued with the warmth I had begun, and I saw that the longer I did this, the more the water disappeared, and the dead bodies, black as coal, came to view. And indeed this would have happened sooner had not the room been locked and sealed so tightly. But under no conditions dared I open it. Then I noticed quite clearly that the water rose high toward the clouds, collected on the ceiling of the room, and descended again like rain; nothing could escape, so our bridegroom lay with his beloved bride before my eyes dead and rotten, stinking beyond all measure. Meanwhile, I saw in the room a rainbow of the most beautiful colors, caused by the sunshine in the moist weather, which heartened me no little in the midst of my sorrows. And soon I became rather happy that I could see my two lovers lying before me.

However, no joy is so great that sorrow is not mixed with it; therefore in my joy I was sorrowful because I saw the ones I was to have guarded lying lifeless before me. But since their room was made from such pure and solid material and was shut so tightly, I knew that their soul and their spirit could not escape, but were still enclosed in it, so I continued with my steady warmth day and night, carrying out my duty as prescribed, for I believed that the two would not return to their bodies so long as the moisture was present. This I indeed found to be true. For in many careful observations I observed that many vapors arose from the earth about evening, through the power of the sun, and ascended on high as if the sun itself were drawing up the water. But during the night they gathered into a lovely and fertile dew, descending very early in the morning, enriching the earth and washing the corpses of our dead, so that from day to day, the longer such bathing and washing continued, they became even whiter and more beautiful. But the more beautiful and whiter they became, the more they lost their moisture, until at last when the air became light and clear and all the foggy, damp weather had passed, the spirit and soul of the bride could no longer remain in the pure air, and returned into the transfigured, glorified body of the Queen, and as soon as the body felt their presence, it instantly became living once again.

This brought me no little joy, as one can easily imagine, especially as I saw her arise, dressed in a very rich garment, the like of which very few on this earth have seen, wearing a costly crown, adorned with perfect diamonds, and heard her say:

"Harken, you children of men, and learn, all of you who are of women born, that the All-Highest has power to enthrone kings and to dethrone them. He makes rich and poor, according to his will. He kills and makes to live again. And all this behold in me as a living example! I was great and I became small. But now after I became humble, I have been made queen over many realms. I was killed and am resurrected again. To me, the poor one, have the great treasures of the wise and mighty been entrusted and given. Therefore have I been given power to make the poor rich, to extend mercy to the humble, and to bring health to the sick. But not yet am I like my dearest brother, the great, mighty king, who will also be awakened from the dead. When he comes he will prove that my words are true."

And as she said this, the sun shone brightly, the days became warmer, and the dog-days were near at hand. But long before the sumptuous and great wedding of our new queen many costly robes were prepared from black velvet, ash-grey colored damask, grey silk, silver-colored taffeta, snow-white satin; indeed, a silver piece of extraordinary beauty, embroidered with costly pearls and worked with marvellous, clear-sparkling diamonds was also made ready. And robes for the young king were also made ready, namely of pink, with yellow aureolin colors, costly fabrics, and finally a red velvet garment adorned with costly rubies and carbuncles in very great numbers. But the tailors who made these garments were invisible, and I marveled when I saw one coat after another, and one garment after another being finished, for I knew that no one except the bridegroom and his bride had entered into the chamber. But what astonished me the most was that as soon as a new coat or garment was finished, the former ones disappeared from before my eyes, and I did not know where they had gone or who had locked them away.

And after this costly coat was made ready, the great and mighty king appeared in all his power and glory, and there was nothing like him. And when he discovered he was locked in, he asked me in a friendly manner and with gracious words to open the door for him so he would be able to come out; he said it would result in great blessing for me. Although I was strictly forbidden to open the room,

I was so overwhelmed by the great appearance and the gentle persuasive powers of the king that I opened the door willingly. And as he walked out, he was so friendly, gracious, even humble, that one could indeed see that nothing graces noble persons so much as do these virtues.

And since he had passed the dog-days in the great heat, he was very thirsty, weak and tired; and he asked me to bring him some of the fast-flowing water from beneath the water-wheels of the mill, which I did, and he drank it with great eagerness. Then he returned to his chamber and told me to lock the door fast behind him, lest someone should disturb him or waken him from his sleep.

There he rested for a few days, and then he called me to open the door. But I saw that he had become much more handsome, full-blooded and splendid, and he also noticed it; and he thought that the water was marvellous and healthy. Therefore he asked for more, and drank a larger quantity than he had the first time, and I resolved to enlarge the chamber. After the king had drunk his fill of this wonderful beverage which the ignorant do not value at all, he became so handsome and glorious that in all my life I never saw a more splendid appearance, or anyone more noble in manner and character. Then he led me into his kingdom and showed me all the treasures and riches of the world, so that I must say that not only did the queen speak the truth, but he also gave the greatest part of it to those who know the treasure and can describe it. There were gold and precious carbuncle stones without end, and the rejuvenation and restoration of the natural powers, as well as the recovery of health and the removal of all illnesses were daily occurrences there. But most delightful of all in this kingdom was that the people knew, reverenced and praised their Creator, receiving from Him wisdom and knowledge, and at last, after this happiness in the world of time, they attained an eternal blessedness. To this may God, Father, Son and Holy Spirit help all of us.

Bibliography

I. Original Editions

Chymische Hochzeit Christiani Rosencreutz, Anno 1459. Strasburg: Lazarus Zetzner, 1616.

The Hermeticke Romance, or *The Chymical Wedding.* Written in High Dutch by C. R., translated by Ezechiel Foxcroft. London, 1690.

II. Later Editions

Allen, Paul. *A Christian Rosenkreutz Anthology.* New York: Rudolph Steiner Books, 1968. Contains the Foxcroft English text with notes by Paul Allen.

Andreae, Johann Valentin. *The Chymical Wedding of Christian Rosenkreutz.* Translated into English by E. Foxcroft. London: Minerva Books, 1982.

Auriger, ed. Modern French edition of the *Chymische Hochzeit,* 1928.

Bennell, Margaret and Wyatt, Isabel. *An Introductory Commentary on The Chymical Wedding of Christian Rosenkreutz.* Hawkwood College, 1965.

Hall, Manly Palmer. *The Secret Teachings of All Ages: An Encyclopaedic Outline of Masonic, Hermetic, Qabbalistic and Rosicrucian Symbolical Philosophy.* California, 1928. Summary and comments in chapter CLXI.

Maack, Ferdinand, ed. *Die Chymischen Hochzeit des Christian Rosenkreutz.* Berlin: Verlag Barsdorf, 1913, 1922.

Montgomery, J. W. *Cross and Crucible: J. V. Andreae (1586–1654).* Phoenix of the Theologians: Vol. I, Andreae's Life, World View, etc.; Vol. II, *The Chemical Wedding,* facsimile of Foxcroft edition with notes and commentary. The Hague: Martinus Nijhoff, 1973.

Van der Stok, Hans. *Contemplations on the Chymical Wedding of Christian Rosenkreutz.* Camphill Press, 1981.

Van Dulmen, Richard. *Fama Fraternitatis, Confessio Fraternitatis, Chymische Hochzeit: Christiani Rosenkreutz, Anno 1459.* Stuttgart, 1973.

Waite, A. E. The *Real History of the Rosicrucians*. London, 1887. Contains an abridged version of the *Chemical Wedding*.

Weber, Walter. *Die Chymische Hochzeit des Christian Rosenkreuz Anno 1459*. With an Essay by Rudolph Steiner. Dornach, 1957; enlarged edition Stuttgart, 1957.

Chymische Hochzeit Christiani Rosencreutz. With 28 drawings by Hans Wildermann. Regensburg, 1923.

The *Chymical Wedding of Christian Rosencreutz*, A modern poetic version of Jon Valentine (pseudonym) with imaginations by Arne Salomonsen. St. George Publications, 1981.

III. Books Contemporary with the *Chymische Hochzeit* of especial relevance

Brotoffer, Radtichs. Elucidarius Major. Luneburg, 1617. (Commentary on the *Chymische Hochzeit*.)

C.V.M.V.S. Practica Leonis *Viridis*. Halle, 1619. (Commentary of days one and two of the *Chymische Hochzeit*.)

Schweighardt, Theophilus. *Speculum Sophicum Rhodo-Stauroticum*. Constantiensem, 1618.

IV. Recent writings of relevance

Hall, Manly Palmer. *Codex Rosae Crucis*. Los Angeles: Philosophical Research Society, 1971.

Jung, C. G. *Psychology and Alchemy*. Bollingen Series XX. Translated by R. F. C. Hull. Princeton: Princeton University Press, 1977.

McIntosh, Christopher. *The Rosy Cross Unveiled*. Wellingborough: Aquarian Press, 1980.

McLean, Adam, ed. *The Amphitheatre Engravings of Heinrich Khunrath*. Magnum Opus Hermetic Sourceworks, No. 7. Originally published Edinburgh, 1981.

McLean, Adam, ed. *A Commentary on Goethe's Fairy Tale*. Magnum Opus Hermetic Sourceworks, No. 14. Originally published Edinburgh, 1982.

Yates, Frances. *The Rosicrucian Enlightenment*. London, 1972.